FAITH AND SCIENCE

"I know of no Christian scholar more competent to write this book than my colleague and friend Ken Keathley. He brings together the minds of a philosopher, a scientist, and a theologian in challenging us to think well about God's marvelous creation. I will be quick to recommend this book. It is superbly done."

—**Daniel L. Akin**, president, Southeastern Baptist Theological Seminary

"Wishing for a biblically faithful book introducing the main themes involving Christian faith and contemporary science? I've waited for one avoiding extremes and confusions; now I've found it. Dr. Keathley treats us with exceptionally clear overviews of all the right issues; it's a major accomplishment in such a concise volume. Though perfect for STEM students, *Faith and Science* is now my first choice for anyone desiring the truth on such vital issues."

—**Theodore J. Cabal**, professor of philosophy of religion, Southwestern Baptist Theological Seminary

"It's a modern myth that a robust Christian faith and the wonders of scientific inquiry are enemies. Ken Keathley offers a needed, necessary guide for those who want to see how these two worlds interact. If you work in scientific disciplines, this will give you fresh confidence that you don't have to check your Christian faith at the lab door. If you are a theologian, you'll find fresh arguments that bolster your faith in the God of the Bible. And for everyone who seeks truth, this is a readable, accessible map to understanding both God's world and God's Word. This is a resource every pastor should have in his library."

—**Daniel Darling**, director of The Land Center for Cultural Engagement, Southwestern Baptist Theological Seminary

"The questions Dr. Ken Keathley deals with in this book are at the heart of our apologetic task. If you are looking for a way to get upstream from on-campus debates so that you can enter them with winsomeness, grace, and erudition, Dr. Keathley is the right man to be your guide. This book is not just thorough; it's easy to understand and fun to read!"

—**J. D. Greear**, pastor, The Summit Church, Raleigh-Durham, North Carolina

"It has been a great privilege to dialogue personally with Dr. Ken Keathley about many things this well-researched and thoughtful book addresses in a way the scholar, the pastor, the laity, and inquiring minds young and old can enjoy and learn from. This book will show you how science—from the big bang to the fine-tuning of the universe—truly is compatible with biblical theology and is a great friend, not a grievous foe, to biblical faith. It is an outstanding contribution to this ongoing conversation that will only end when time does."

—**James Merritt**, senior pastor,
Cross Pointe Church, Duluth, Georgia

"Ken Keathley has written an engaging and encouraging primer on the interrelationship between faith and science. He shows, through historical and contemporary examples, that one need not abandon the faith to appreciate science. He also demonstrates that science alone is insufficient to make sense of this world. We live in a hypernatural world that is best explained by an active God who created and sustains everything in it. I will be recommending this biblically faithful and well-researched book to students and church members for years to come."

—**Andrew J. Spencer**, senior research fellow for
the Institute of Faith, Work, and Economics

"It's remarkable to see recent scientific inquiries and discoveries that align with the biblical teaching that God created the world out of nothing. Ken Keathley brings readers up to speed on new developments in different spheres of study as well as the various models adopted by Christians grappling with different views on how best to explain God's design of the world. A simple and helpful introduction to an ongoing conversation."

—**Trevin Wax**, vice president for research and resource
development, North American Mission Board

"Exercising rock-solid biblical conviction and Christlike humility, Kenneth Keathley has accomplished what most intellectuals considered impossible after Darwin and Hodge took up their gloves. Our professor demonstrates through careful scientific evaluation coupled with pristine theological orthodoxy that diverse approaches to truth need not remain in perpetual unedifying conflict. *Faith and Science* will become the leading primer on creation for believers and unbelievers alike, in the academy and in the workplace, because it shows how Christians can reason lovingly and convincingly with all who hunger for truth. I wholeheartedly recommend this exceptionally accessible masterpiece."

—**Malcolm B. Yarnell III**, research professor of
theology, Southwestern Baptist Theological Seminary

FAITH AND SCIENCE

a primer for a hypernatural world

KENNETH KEATHLEY

B&H ACADEMIC®
BRENTWOOD, TENNESSEE

Faith and Science: A Primer for a Hypernatural World
Copyright © 2024 by Kenneth Keathley

Published by B&H Academic®
Brentwood, Tennessee

All rights reserved.

ISBN: 978-1-0877-7143-4

Dewey Decimal Classification: 215
Subject Heading: BIBLE AND SCIENCE \ RELIGION AND SCIENCE \ SCIENCE

Unless otherwise noted, all Scripture quotations are taken from the Christian Standard Bible®, Copyright © 2017 by Holman Bible Publishers. Used by permission. Christian Standard Bible® and CSB® are federally registered trademarks of Holman Bible Publishers.

The web addresses referenced in this book were live and correct at the time of the book's publication but may be subject to change.

Cover design by Julian Davis. Collage images sourced from: Morphart Creation/Shutterstock, Lauritta/Shutterstock, RockStocks/DeviantArt, Adi Ulitski/Behance, Alek Po/Vecteezy, fahrulsaputra/Vecteezy, and Spazierweg/KindPNG.

Printed in the United States of America

29 28 27 26 25 24 VP 1 2 3 4 5 6 7 8 9 10

CONTENTS

ACKNOWLEDGMENTS

Writing this primer has been an adventure, and like any good adventure, it's the people along the way who make it truly special. Huge thanks go out to Benjamin Quinn and Jeff Zweerink for being my dialogue partners and for their input, advice, and comments. I must thank Penny, my wife, for being a long-suffering sounding board for so many of my thoughts and ideas. A special shout-out also to Steve Ladd, who was a beacon of clarity in the exploration of complex narratives. Their insights were gold; any missteps along the way are on me.

I'm grateful to the administration and trustees of Southeastern Baptist Theological Seminary—my teaching home—for granting me a sabbatical in order to write this primer. Funding was also provided by a generous grant from the John Templeton Foundation.

And then there's the wonderful crew at the L. Russ Bush Center for Faith and Culture. You guys kept the ship sailing smoothly while I was tucked away in my office, buried in this project. Lisa McKneely, Megan Dickerson, Nathaniel Williams, and Rachel Smith, you're the real MVPs. Your hard work made it possible for me to focus on bringing this primer to life, and for that, I'm grateful. You're the best, seriously.

INTRODUCTION

This Is Our Father's Hypernatural World

Whenever we look up at the night sky, dive into the mysteries of the human body, or even play around with the coolest new tech gadget, we are reminded that we're living in a world that's full of wonders—our Father's world. The story of faith and science isn't a narrative about two worlds clashing. Rather it's a tale of discovering that the better we understand the cosmos, the more we realize the intricate way that God has crafted it. This little book is an invitation to explore that story, a story of divine wonder and human curiosity.

The first three chapters set the stage. Chapter 1, "How Do Faith and Science Relate to Each Other," helps us to tackle the big questions of how and why things are the way they are and how faith and science can have an ongoing conversation with each other. Chapter 2, "Christianity and the Scientific Revolution," explains how Christianity isn't the enemy of science; rather, the Christian faith provided the essential conceptual framework when the big scientific discoveries were just starting. Chapter 3, "How Does God Involve Himself in the World?" dives into the idea of hypernaturalism. It explores the spectrum of God's interaction with his creation, from the routine orchestration of natural laws to the rare, wondrous occurrence of miracles and the hypernatural instances where divine providence is exceptionally manifest. We must distinguish between the different ways God interacts with his creation—from the everyday natural stuff to the show-stopping miracles and the hypernatural moments, where God's special touch is like a hidden track in the soundtrack of reality.

Chapters 4–8 explore various exemplars of the hypernatural—places and instances in the cosmos where the divine signature is intricately engraved on the canvas of nature. We will look at (1) the big bang, (2) the meticulous fine-tuning of the universe, (3) the surprisingly rare qualities of our planet that enable life to exist, (4) the enigmatic, mysterious question of the origin of life on earth, and (5) the complex, hypernatural choreography in the realm of biology. Each of these chapters argues that science itself unveils the hypernatural, sublime artistry of God.

Last, chapter 9 is written to young believers considering a future in one of the STEM fields. The Bible calls us to view the world through a Christ-centered lens. The chapter examines what it means to be a disciple of Christ, serving him in the realms of science, technology, engineering, or mathematics. It urges a joyful and confident exploration of the natural world, by which, the Christ-follower partakes in the grand narrative of unveiling the majestic tapestry of God's creation.

As you journey through the pages of this primer, may your faith be enriched, your scientific curiosity be invigorated, and your commitment to Christ be strengthened. "The heavens declare the glory of God, and the expanse proclaims the work of his hands" (Ps 19:1). In every inquiry and in every revelation, may you find a fresh invitation to stand in awe, to worship, and to delve deeper into the boundless wonder of our Father's world.

1

How Do Faith and Science Relate to Each Other?

Distinguishing between How and Why

Why does it rain? When I ask this question of students, typically one of them gives a good explanation of the cycle of evaporation, condensation, and precipitation. The sun heats the oceans, seas, and lakes, causing water to evaporate. As the evaporated water rises higher in the atmosphere, it cools, causing it to condense into liquid form. Gathering as clouds, the condensed water falls back to earth as rain.

But that answer does not explain why it rains. Rather it explains how. We often get the two types of questions confused, especially in our technological age. Today we think that if the cause-and-effect processes of a phenomenon are grasped then all the really important questions about it have been answered. However, this misses the point of the "why" question. Switching examples, consider a teakettle. Explaining the convection processes that heat it up does not explain why a teakettle boils, only how it boils. So why does the kettle boil? Because I want a cup of tea.

The Four Different Ways to Understand "Cause"

The teakettle example highlights the ambiguity surrounding the notion of "cause." Since the days of ancient Greece, philosophers have noted four main ways to understand causation: formal, material, efficient, and final. *Formal causation* is what gives a thing its form (hence the word "formal"). A formal cause is the plan that gives something its shape or essential features. *Material causation* is when something has the materials it needs to exist. For example, a chair needs wood, nails, and glue to become a chair. *Efficient causation* is the thing that causes something to happen. For example, if you press a button, it can make the lights turn on. The pressing of the button efficiently caused the lights to light up. *Final causation* is the reason something happens. It's the goal that is being worked toward, like boiling water in a teakettle to make a cup of tea.

Here is an analogy that may help. Think of a new house under construction. The blueprints that guide the construction are the formal cause of the house. The lumber, concrete, shingles, and other stuff are the material causes of the house. The carpenters, roofers, and construction workers are the efficient causes of the house. And the desire to have a place to raise your family is the final cause. All four forms of causation come together when the home is being built.

As the analogy illustrates, formal cause and final cause address the "why" of something, while material cause and efficient cause deal with the "how." Formal cause and final cause are the plan and purpose of something. Material cause and efficient cause address what something is and how it came to be. So how does this apply to relating science and faith? Science focuses on efficient and material causes, while faith addresses the formal and final causes. Science and faith both look at the universe God created, but they ask different questions. It doesn't mean that their questions are not related or that they don't overlap, but it does mean that their respective questions are distinct and have different emphases. Science studies creation to understand what the world is and the processes that bring everything about. Faith explores God's plan and purposes for the world. Science studies the "how." Faith seeks to understand the "why."

Defining Faith and Science

Recently I saw a fellow wearing a T-shirt that said, "Science is real!"[1] I think I know the point he was trying to make, but the statement is a bit confusing. Science is not real in the sense that persons, places, and things are *real*. However, the slogan helps to highlight one of the problems facing discussions about faith and science—the use of multiple definitions and the tendency to equivocate between them.

Both *faith* and *science* can be defined three ways: (1) as a methodology, (2) as a body of knowledge, and (3) as an institution.

---

[1] This section of the chapter is based on my article, "The Ethics of Integrating Faith and Science," *Religions* 14, no. 5 (Spring 2023), https://www.mdpi.com/2077-1444/14/5/644.

In other words, each can be understood in terms of what it is, what it does, and who does it. The third way of understanding science—as an institution—seems to be often overlooked, and we will explore it further in "Defining Science."

Each of the three approaches to formulating a definition has problems. For instance, neither faith nor science uses just one methodology or approach to knowing, and neither marks a clear boundary for the range of the body of knowledge that it claims. Similarly, the institutional communities engaged in the process of gathering and affirming the respective bodies of knowledge are complex, variegated, and multileveled. Therefore, these definitions will have to be simply working definitions, approximations that have exceptions and caveats; but they should operate sufficiently for the task at hand.

Defining Faith

Let's start with a definition of faith. First, I don't mean religion or all faiths in general. The *faith*—the body of knowledge—I have in mind is the *Christian faith* as expressed in the Apostle's Creed. Those who affirm the triune God and the saving work of Jesus Christ are brethren, walking together on the journey of faith. For the purposes of this book, faith refers to the body of beliefs that could be held by someone who affirms what C. S. Lewis called "mere Christianity," though I personally write from the perspective of someone who affirms the Chicago Statement on Biblical Inerrancy.[2]

[2] Chicago Statement on Biblical Inerrancy, https://www.sebts.edu/wp-content/uploads/2022/10/chicago-statement-on-biblical-inerrancy.pdf.

Second, the Christian faith can be defined by the way it collects and organizes its beliefs. *Theology* is the attempt to understand and summarize what God has revealed. God reveals himself to us through nature, through Scripture, and most of all through his Son, Jesus Christ. Theology explores the treasure trove of God's truth—using tradition, reason, and experience—with the Bible acting as our ultimate authority. So faith can be defined by its methodology.

Third, this endeavor of knowing and categorizing divine truth isn't a solo expedition but rather is a group adventure within a community. This *community* is the church—a divine yet human institution. Despite its human flaws, the church—guided by the infallible Bible, the Holy Spirit, and God's providence—continues its journey, tripping at times but always moving forward.

For the purposes of this book, faith refers to (1) the historic beliefs of the church, (2) as understood by theology, and (3) as universally received by the church at large.

Defining Science

Defining science is a surprisingly challenging task, thanks to its vast landscape and the heated debates about what counts as science and what doesn't.[3] Let's tackle it in three bites similar

[3] James C. Zimring, *What Science Is and How It Really Works* (Cambridge: Cambridge University Press, 2019). Zimring argues that a universal definition of science doesn't exist: "Despite the weight that the label of science may carry with many people, it is an utter fiction that there is (or ever has been) a uniform consensus among scientists (or anyone else for that matter) as to what precisely defines science. This question has been tackled over the years by many great

to the ones taken to define faith. This will help us understand what science is, what it does, and who does it.

First, science can be defined as the study of the natural world. Science is all about cracking the code of the natural world. However, this definition can be too restrictive as it overlooks disciplines historically deemed scientific. For example, theology used to be considered the queen of the sciences. Personally, I still think that. Today the term *science* generally refers to natural sciences, such as astronomy, geology, chemistry, and biology. Second, science is a method of learning, chiefly through observation and experimentation. Yet the precise methodologies are debatable because no universal method is accepted across all scientific fields. Some, such as Paul Feyerabend, argue that science can't be defined in terms of method because there is no one-size-fits-all method.[4] Still, the "scientific method" is a broadly recognized trait of science.

---

scholars and yet there is not a clear and unequivocal answer" (p. 3). For other philosophers of science who agree with Zimring's assessment, see James Ladyman, *Understanding Philosophy of Science* (Oxfordshire: Routledge, 2001), 1; and Gijsbert Van den Brink, *Philosophy of Science for Theologians: An Introduction* (Frankfurt: Peter Lang, 2009), 25–29.

[4] See, for example, Paul Feyerabend, *Against Method* (London: Bloomsbury, 2010), 6.

In James C. Zimring's *What Science Is* (see previous footnote), Zimring explains, "For the reasons just stated, most modern attempts at defining science have focused on *methods* or *modes of thinking* that distinguish scientific activities from nonscientific activities rather than the specific content of scientific knowledge claims. However, while one often encounters discussions of 'the scientific method' and its application to investigation, there is a lack of agreement about what precisely this method entails, and there are

Third, science is an institution. One hundred fifty years ago, science was a "gentleman's hobby," a pastime reserved only for the wealthy classes and nobility. It has evolved into an enormous institution thanks largely to efforts by individuals like Thomas Huxley. Huxley was an ardent defender of Charles Darwin's theory of evolution. He saw the debates over evolution as an opportunity to establish science as a fully funded, stand-alone profession.[5] By all measures he succeeded. This institutional facet of science, hosted primarily within universities, is a human endeavor and thus carries the inherent imperfections of humanity. Even if a picture-perfect definition of science remains a bit elusive, we can get a decent grasp by seeing it as (1) a highly specialized area of learning, (2) a focused area of study, and (3) a vast human institution.

The Three Models for Relating Faith and Science

With these working definitions, we can now look at the three primary models for relating faith and science, as presented by a philosopher of science. Ian Barbour has demonstrated that people typically understand faith and science to be either enemies, strangers, or friends.[6]

---

those who argue that the very notion of a scientific method is itself an utter myth" (p. 6).

[5] See Ruth Barton, "'An Influential Set of Chaps': The X-Club and Royal Society Politics 1864–85," *The British Journal for the History of Science* 23, no. 1 (March 1990): 53–81.

[6] Ian Barbour, *When Science Meets Religion: Strangers, Enemies, or Partners* (New York: HarperOne, 2000).

The Enemies Model

The "enemies model," often termed as the conflict or warfare model, initially emerged during the Enlightenment, gaining prominence in the Victorian era. Two significant publications, *History of the Conflict between Religion and Science* (1874) by John William Draper and *A History of the Warfare of Science with Theology in Christendom* (1896) by Andrew Dickson White, laid down the framework of this conflicting narrative. The aforementioned Thomas Huxley, known as "Darwin's Bulldog," embodied the enemies model, famously drawing a parallel between theologians and "strangled snakes" with the words, "Extinguished theologians lie about the cradle of every science as the strangled snakes beside that of Hercules; and history records that whenever science and orthodoxy have been fairly opposed, the latter has been forced to retire from the lists, bleeding and crushed, if not annihilated; scotched if not slain."[7]

Fast forward to today, and it's rare to stumble upon a serious philosopher or a historian of science who champions the conflict model. However, the enemies model hasn't faded away; it's alive and kicking in popular culture and, dishearteningly, among a significant number of individuals immersed in the STEM fields.

On the flip side, in theological circles, some evangelicals confuse the Protestant endorsement of *sola Scriptura* with a simplistic biblicism. They interpret the doctrine of Scripture's sufficiency as a sign that Christians should steer clear of the

---

[7] Thomas H. Huxley, "The Origin of Species," in *Lay Sermons, Addresses, and Reviews* (London: MacMillan, 1860), https://www.gutenberg.org/files/16729/16729-h/16729-h.htm.

wisdom offered by tradition, reason, and experience. This camp also sees any effort to bridge the gap between faith and science as a slippery slope, fearing it might lead to forsaking biblical authority.

The Strangers Model

Ian Barbour presents a second approach, the "strangers model," which he also calls the "independence model." This viewpoint avoids conflict between faith and science by keeping them separate in "watertight compartments."[8] Paleontologist Stephen Jay Gould referred to this approach as "Non-Overlapping Magisteria" (NOMA). Gould argued that faith and science cannot conflict because they operate in entirely distinct domains.[9] Science provides facts; religion expresses values. Never the twain shall meet.

Scientists are not the only ones to advocate the strangers model. It can also be seen in the work of some of the preeminent theologians of the twentieth century such as Karl Barth, Paul Tillich, and Reinhold Niebuhr. From reading their works, one could get the impression that science didn't exist. They "virtually ignored science in their theological writing."[10]

---

[8] Barbour, *When Science Meets Religion,* 27.

[9] Stephen Jay Gould, *Rocks of Ages: Science and Religion in the Fullness of Life* (New York: Ballantine, 1999). A current advocate of the strangers model would be Michael Ruse. See Michael Ruse, "Independence View," in *Three Views on Christianity and Science*, ed. Paul Copan and Christopher Reece (Grand Rapids, MI: Zondervan, 2021).

[10] Edward J. Larson and Michael Ruse, *On Faith and Science* (New Haven, CT: Yale University Press, 2017), 11.

Barth's *Church Dogmatics* is over six million words long, yet he never finds space to discuss science.

Advocates of the strangers model are correct when they point out the distinctions between faith and science. Faith and science have different frames of reference, different lines of enquiry, and different methodologies. But it does not follow that they have no areas of overlap or engagement. In fact, it is generally recognized that the opposite is true. As we will see in chapter 3, it is a historical fact that Christianity provided the conceptual, epistemological, and ontological frameworks for modern science as a discipline.[11] The Christian faith gave the moral sanction for doing science and still provides the ethical norms for how science should be conducted. Not only do science and faith interact—they do so necessarily. Which brings us to the friends model.

---

[11] Historians of science have provided a remarkable body of work that overwhelmingly demonstrates this point. A sampling would be David C. Lindberg, *The Beginnings of Western Science: The European Scientific Tradition in Philosophical, Religious, and Institutional Context, 600 B.C. to A.D. 1450* (Chicago: University of Chicago, 1992); Nancy Pearcey and Charles Thaxton, *The Soul of Science: Christian Faith and Natural Philosophy* (Wheaton, IL: Crossway, 1994); Toby E. Huff, *The Rise of Early Modern Science: Islam, China, and the West* (Cambridge: Cambridge University Press, 2003); Peter Harrison, *The Fall of Man and the Foundations of Science* (Cambridge: Cambridge University Press, 2009); James Hannam, *The Genesis of Science: How the Christian Middle Ages Launched the Scientific Revolution* (Washington, DC: Regnery, 2011); and James Ungureanu, *Science, Religion and the Protestant Tradition: Retracing the Origins of Conflict* (Pittsburgh: University of Pittsburgh Press, 2019).

The Friends Model

Throughout the history of the church, the majority of Christians have affirmed some version of the friends model. This model begins with the opening claim of the Bible: the God who reveals himself in Scripture is the same God who created the heavens and the earth. Both realms—Scripture and nature—reveal God but in different ways. This twofold revelation is often called the "two books metaphor" and is expressed beautifully by the Belgic Confession:

> First, by the creation, preservation and government of the universe; which is before our eyes as a most beautiful book, wherein all creatures, great and small, are as so many letters leading us to contemplate clearly the invisible qualities of God, namely His eternal power and divine nature, as the apostle Paul says in Rom 1:20. All these things are sufficient to convict men and leave them without excuse. Second, He makes Himself more clearly and fully known to us by His holy and divine Word as far as is necessary for us in this life, to His glory and our salvation.[12]

In affirming the "two books metaphor," the Confession follows the clear teaching of Scripture that there is a general revelation in nature and a special revelation in the Bible (Psalm 19; Acts 14:15–17; 17:24–28; Romans 1). The friends model attempts to properly relate the two modes of revelation. This involves the

[12] The Belgic Confession, article 2, https://www.prca.org/bc_text1.html#a2.

careful study and interpretation of both. Today we call the careful study of God's creation the "natural sciences."

There are limits to both fields of study. On the one hand, science can tell us how the universe works, but it cannot tell us what it all means. On the other hand, the Christian faith tells us what it means but typically does not tell us how it works. As C. S. Lewis puts it, "Christianity does *not* replace the technical. When it tells you to feed the hungry it doesn't give you lessons in cooking. If you want to learn *that*, you must go to a cook rather than a Christian."[13] To give another example, the Bible tells us that the universe was created *ex nihilo*, out of nothing. It doesn't tell us that it happened 13.787 billion years ago as revealed by the Planck telescope data.[14] Evangelicals almost universally affirm some version of the friends model. However, sometimes conservative evangelicals tend to veer into the enemies model, while more progressive evangelicals at times flirt with the strangers model.[15]

---

[13] C. S. Lewis, *God in the Dock* (Grand Rapids, MI: Eerdmans, 2014), 36.

[14] N. Aghamin et al., "Planck 2018 Results," *Astronomy and Astrophysics* (September 2020): 641, https://doi.org/10.1051/0004-6361/201833910.

[15] Henry Morris and Ken Ham are examples of the former, while Peter Enns and Karl Giberson are examples of the latter. See Henry Morris, *The Long War Against God: The History and Impact of the Evolution/Creation Conflict* (Green Forest, AR: Master Books, 2000); Ken Ham, *The Lie: Evolution* (Green Forest, AR: Master Books, 1987); Peter Enns, *The Evolution of Adam: What the Bible Says and Doesn't Say about Evolution* (Grand Rapids, MI: Brazos, 2012); and Karl Giberson, *Saving the Original Sinner: The Christians Have Used the Bible's First Man to Oppress, Inspire, and Make Sense of the World* (Boston: Beacon, 2015). I am not saying that all young-earth creationists (YEC) adhere to the enemies model, nor am I saying that

An Arguendo Approach

Time for me to put all my cards on the table. I hold to old-earth creationism (OEC). When most read or hear "creationist," they assume that I believe a faithful reading of Genesis requires the belief that the universe is less than 10,000 years old. That position is actually young-earth creationism (YEC). By and large I accept the empirical findings of the natural sciences—astronomy, geology, and biology. But I push back at those who wish to make metaphysical claims in the name of science. So, I have no problem accepting the standard interpretation of the geological column, but I don't accept the standard Darwinian explanation for it. It concerns me that by revealing my position I might turn off two types of readers that I hope will give me a hearing. On the one hand, my YEC reader probably thinks I'm in danger of compromise. On the other hand, my Darwinian reader may dismiss me as a quaint Luddite. Please don't put down the book just yet.

This book takes an *arguendo* approach. This was a favorite tactic of Francis Schaeffer, the twentieth-century apologist, and he used it to great effect. He called the arguendo approach "the middle way" or "taking the roof off."[16] When he talked to a skeptic, he would, for the sake of argument, assume the skeptic's

---

all evolutionary creationists (EC) hold to the strangers model. Some YEC advocates, such as Marcus Ross and Todd Wood, display a deep love for science, while some EC proponents, such as Darrel Falk, Jeff Schloss, Jeff Hardin, and Michael Murray, care deeply about theological commitments.

[16] William Edgar, "Two Christian Warriors: Cornelius Van Til and Francis A. Schaeffer Compared," *Westminster Theological Journal* 57, no. 1 (Spring 1995): 57–80.

worldview. Then Schaeffer would logically walk with the skeptic through that worldview's natural conclusion.

What is an arguendo approach? An arguendo approach means that, without endorsing a position, I will argue from the claims of that position. We are going to look at the big bang, the fine-tuning argument, the Rare Earth hypothesis, and more. So, in this book, I ask the reader—who may be a YEC or Darwinian evolutionist—to consider the arguments at face value. This approach is similar to what some call "honest disagreement." As one philosopher explains, "Honest disagreement involves a certain attitude that presupposes that one's opponent is possibly right and willing to consider the arguments for his position without preconceived bias or animus against them."[17] In chapter 3, I set out the case for "hypernaturalism," a view that argues that God at times employs natural law and natural phenomena in an extraordinary way to bring about his will. A hypernatural event is the point at which providence and miracles intersect.

My hope is that by taking an arguendo approach, I can help readers see how well the Christian faith meshes with the scientific enterprise—or, if it turns out that faith and science don't mesh, what needs to be modified. This book is my attempt to take off the roof and explore issues such as creationism and evolution as honestly as I can—all under the lordship of Jesus Christ. It's a tall task, but I'm convinced it is an important one.

---

[17] Source unknown.

2

Christianity and the Scientific Revolution

As we noted in the last chapter, some see faith and science existing in a state of constant conflict. Even though today few historians or philosophers of science hold such a view, at a popular level and among the "new atheists," the conflict metaphor still prevails. History presents a very different story. Contrary to the enemies model, the relationship between the Christian faith and science has historically been one of fruitful dialogue and interaction. More important, doctrines from the Bible supplied many of the elements necessary for the rise and flourishing of science. Rather than being an impediment, the Christian worldview was the matrix from which the Scientific Revolution was birthed.

Two Serious Misfires

Despite the fact that Christianity played a crucial role in the formation of science, there have been some serious misfires.

Two of the most obvious (which unfortunately get a great deal of attention) are often referred to as the Galileo Affair and the Scopes Monkey Trial; however, these were not simply examples of faith versus science. In both instances the story is much more complex.

The Galileo Affair

In 1633 the Inquisition of the Roman Catholic Church condemned Galileo Galilei (1564–1642) for teaching that the earth went around the sun rather than the sun going around the earth. The Church endorsed the established Ptolemaic system (which put the earth at the center of the solar system) and rejected the new heliocentric model that had been first proposed by Nicolaus Copernicus (1473–1543) and later advocated by Galileo.

This seems to be a cut-and-dried case of religious bigotry oppressing scientific inquiry, but things were a bit more complicated than that. As astronomer Owen Gingerich points out, at the time the Ptolemaic system and the Copernican system worked equally well in predicting planetary motion.[1] So the advantages to the Copernican system were not immediately obvious. Second, prior to the incident with Galileo, both Protestant and Catholic authorities had little problem with the scholarly debate about the heliocentric model. Pope Urban VIII gave his tacit approval to the heliocentric system being taught as a possible model and even supported Galileo financially.

---

[1] Owen Gingerich, "The Copernican Revolution," in *Science and Religion: A Historical Introduction*, ed. Gary B. Ferngren (Baltimore: Johns Hopkins University Press, 2002), 96–97.

All that changed when Galileo published a book that lampooned the pope. Pope Urban's friendship turned to anger, and eventually Galileo was condemned to house arrest. This was a case of politics, not religion, triumphing over science. That doesn't make the Church's behavior any less inexcusable, but it does clarify what the conflict truly was. In this matter, Galileo was not only the better scientist, but he was also the better theologian. When he famously observed, "The intention of the Holy Ghost is to teach us how one goes to heaven, not how heaven goes," he was undoubtedly correct.[2]

The Scopes Monkey Trial

Centuries after the debacle with Galileo, a similar disaster occurred, this time over Darwin's theory of evolution. In 1925, the state of Tennessee made it illegal for the theory of evolution to be taught in public schools. As a publicity stunt, the leaders of the town of Dayton, Tennessee, orchestrated a show trial to challenge the law, with celebrity lawyers for both the prosecution and the defense. A schoolteacher, John T. Scopes (1900–1970), agreed to be the defendant, even though he was a football coach who had never taught biology, much less the theory of evolution. Well-known politician and three-time candidate for the presidency of the United States, William Jennings Bryan (1860–1925), volunteered to prosecute the case. Clarence Darrow (1857–1938), a famous defense attorney, provided the

[2] Galileo Galilei, "Letter to Madame Christina of Lorraine, Grand Duchess of Tuscany," 1615, *Interdisciplinary Encyclopedia of Religion and Science*, accessed November 28, 2023, https://inters.org/galilei-madame-christina-Lorraine.

defense for Scopes. The case, from beginning to end, was more of a circus than a trial and came to be known as the Scopes Monkey Trial.

Typically, the Scopes trial is presented as the classic case of creationism versus evolution. As with the Galileo affair, the truth is more complicated. For instance, in many ways Bryan was not conservative, much less a fundamentalist. Politically he was a progressive—each time he ran for president he did so on the Democratic ticket. He was not a young-earth creationist, nor did he interpret the creation account of Genesis as six literal days. In fact, in private Bryan acknowledged that he was comfortable with the notion of non-human evolution.[3]

What motivated Bryan to be so adamantly anti-evolution was the rise of a movement called Social Darwinism. Social Darwinists used Darwin's theory of evolution to justify a "survival of the fittest" approach to society and culture. Often Social Darwinists advocated fascism, racism, imperialism, and eugenics. Bryan was alarmed by Social Darwinism and believed that the movement had to be attacked at it roots. The rise of Nazism in Germany and of eugenics in America (including the forced sterilizations of thousands of infirm and minority persons) during the 1930s showed that Bryan's concerns about Social Darwinism were not unfounded. Technically, Bryan and the prosecution won the Scopes trial. However, the press had a field day lampooning "Bible-thumping" literalists. In the court of public opinion, creationism was considered to have been discredited.

---

[3] Ronald Numbers, *The Creationists: From Scientific Creationism to Intelligent Design,* expanded ed. (Cambridge, MA: Harvard University Press, 2006), 58.

The Scientific Revolution

The Galileo Affair and the Scopes Monkey Trial were tragic episodes that Christians should keep in mind. The good news is that not only are those episodes not the whole story; they are not even a large part of the story. The real story is that Christian scientists played an integral role in bringing about the Scientific Revolution. Consider the following list of men: Nicolaus Copernicus, Johannes Kepler, Rene Descartes, Galileo Galilei, Robert Boyle, Gottfried Leibnitz, Sir Isaac Newton, Robert Hooke, Blaise Pascal, Michael Faraday, Lord Kelvin, James Clerk Maxwell, Gregor Mendel, and Louis Pasteur. They all have two things in common—they are considered the founders of modern science, and they were all men of faith.

What Was the Scientific Revolution?

The Scientific Revolution was a period of intense scientific discovery and innovation from the mid-sixteenth century to the late-eighteenth century. It began in earnest in 1543 with Nicolaus Copernicus's proposal that the earth revolved around the sun. Copernicus's model was confirmed by the groundbreaking discoveries and advances made by brilliant thinkers such as Johannes Kepler, Galileo Galilei, and Isaac Newton. Just as important as their discoveries was the new, more rigorous approach to studying the natural world—the scientific method.

As noted in the previous chapter, the scientific method utilizes careful, systematic processes to investigate and gain understanding of the natural world. It involves the collection of data through observation and experimentation, and the formulation and testing of hypotheses. Scientific knowledge is acquired through careful analysis of data collected from the physical world. Scientific method relies heavily on observation and experimentation.

Occasionally one can come across the expression "ancient science," but this is an anachronism. Science as we understand it today was not practiced in the ancient world. This is not to say that they weren't curious about the cosmos or that they didn't study the world. Our ancient ancestors developed a remarkable amount of technical know-how and craftsmanship. But science, as a well-defined discipline and methodology, did not fully come into its own until the seventeenth and eighteenth centuries.

Since we're talking about misleading expressions, the very expression "scientific revolution" is also more than a little misleading. The word *revolution* gives the idea of something radical and sudden. But historians of science tell us that science as a discipline developed gradually throughout the late medieval period. So rather than being a radical break with the past, the Scientific Revolution was more the natural progression of the discoveries and methodologies developed over the previous centuries. Copernicus's theory marked a clear break with the Ptolemaic system that had dominated for over a millennium, but Copernicus built on the progress that was being made at the time. The sixteenth and seventeenth centuries were indeed revolutionary times, but that had as much to do with the social, political, and economic upheavals as it had with the rise of science.

Why Did the Scientific Revolution Happen in Europe?

Historians of science often raise the question: Why sixteenth-century Europe? A look at the social and economic situation in Europe at that time shows that it is far from obvious that the Scientific Revolution should occur then and there. Other cultures of approximately the same time—Chinese, Muslim, and even Aztec—had better technology, superior economic resources, and greater social stability. Yet none of these cultures was able to bring about what we call the scientific method. Europe enjoyed something that the rest of the world did not: a Christian view of the universe. It's neither an accident nor incidental that Copernicus, Kepler, Galileo, and Newton were all committed believers. A proper understanding of the nature of creation was necessary for the advent of science. Thus, it was Christian Europe of the Renaissance and the Reformation that birthed the Scientific Revolution. What did the Christian worldview provide? Historians of science note four features.

The Concept of the "Uni-verse"

The Christian worldview teaches that nature has order. The ancient pagans believed in many gods, so they had no reason to believe that the universe is controlled by only one set of laws. By contrast, the Bible presents a single transcendent Creator, whose handiwork is a unified, coherent universe.

The ancient pagans were polytheists—they believed in the existence of many gods. As a result, they lived in a kaleidoscope world. Reality seemed to them to be magical, fractured, and disjointed. In 2 Kings 5, the Old Testament provides an interesting example of the polytheist's worldview. Naaman, an officer in the Syrian army (Israel's traditional enemy), was afflicted with leprosy. In desperation he traveled to Israel, and there he asked the prophet Elisha to heal him. Miraculously, after Naaman followed the ritual prescribed by Elisha, his leprosy disappeared. As he was about to return to Syria, Naaman made a very strange request. He asked for two mule loads of dirt (v. 17). Why ask for dirt? After being healed, Naaman wished to worship Israel's god, but he still thought like a pagan. He thought that YAHWEH had power only in Israel. Naaman believed he could commune with Israel's god only while kneeling on Israeli soil.

Fast-forward to seventeenth-century England, where Sir Isaac Newton was contemplating why an apple falls to the ground. He suddenly had a flash of insight when he realized that the force that draws the apple to the earth is the same force that keeps the moon in its orbit. This force—gravity—is universal. How was Newton able to make this logical jump? Because Newton was a Christian holding to a Christian worldview—a worldview that said there is one universal Lawgiver who rules everything by one set of universal laws. This is the advantage Newton had over Naaman: Newton lived in a "uni-verse," a unified world, while Naaman lived with a fractured, disjointed sense of reality. Naaman had a parochial understanding of gods, including Israel's god. Each deity had its respective realm, and each realm had its separate rules and order. Pagans such as Naaman had no reason to believe there was a universal set of properties and relations that governed all of reality.

The Old Testament prophets emphasized this point over and over again: Israel's God is not just a local deity. He is the transcendent Creator of all heaven and earth. The writers of the Old Testament never wearied of making this point, often poking fun at the silly way that pagans thought. For example, in 1 Kings 20 the pagan kings thought that the reason they couldn't defeat Israel was because they were fighting in the mountains and Israel's god(s) were "gods of the mountains." Their solution was to fight down on the lowlands, where they thought Israel's deity or deities (they couldn't tell which) would be powerless. The biblical author recounts, with no small amusement, that the pagan kings found out the hard way that Israel's God ruled the lowlands too.

Today the polytheist's view of reality seems to us to be bizarre and almost quaint, but the pagan worldview acted as a roadblock to seeing science as a unified approach to the world. Even Aristotle did not believe the sun, planets, and stars followed the same laws of nature that govern earth. Christian thinkers, from Newton to Descartes, had no such impediment. They were able to see the created world as a "uni-verse" that obeyed the universal laws set up by the One who is sovereign Creator of all. The Christian worldview of a unified universe was essential for the founding of science.

The Concept of the Laws of Nature

The belief that one God created all of the cosmos leads naturally to the idea of the "laws of nature"—that the Divine Lawgiver assigned the properties and relations that govern cause and effect in the universe. As physicist Paul Davies explains:

> It is not hard to discover where this picture of physical laws comes from: it is inherited directly from monotheism, which asserts that a rational being designed the universe according to a set of perfect laws. And the asymmetry between immutable laws and contingent states mirrors the asymmetry between God and

> nature: the universe depends utterly on God for its existence, whereas God's existence does not depend on the universe.[4]

Consider Asian cultures during the Middle Ages. The Chinese invented gunpowder, the compass, and even printed books. But even though the Chinese were technologically superior to medieval Europe, they had no concept of natural law. As Pearcey and Thaxton explain, "There was no confidence that the code of Nature's laws could be unveiled and read, because there was no assurance that a divine being, even more rational than ourselves, had ever formulated such a code capable of being read."[5] Thus several Asian cultures had technology but not science.

The Concept of God's Freedom

As we've noted, the Christian worldview teaches that nature is subservient to God. He created the universe *ex nihilo* (out of nothing) and hence has absolute control over it. This idea was alien to the ancient world. In all other religions, the creation of the world begins with some kind of preexisting substance with its own inherent nature. As a result, in the pagan religions the creator is not absolute and does not have the freedom to mold the world exactly as he wills. The Christian view of God is that

---

[4] Paul Davies, "Universe from Bit," in *Information and the Nature of Reality: From Physics to Metaphysics,* ed. Paul Davies and Niels Henrik Gregersen (Cambridge: Cambridge University Press, 2014), 90.

[5] Quoting Joseph Needham in Nancy Pearcey and Charles Thaxton, *The Soul of Science: Christian Faith and Natural Philosophy* (Wheaton, IL: Crossway, 1994), 29.

he is sovereign over all creation and thus has the freedom to do whatever he wants in creation.

This view of divine freedom played a crucial part in the development of the scientific method. In 1620, Francis Bacon (1561–1626) published *Novum Organum* ("New Method"). He argued that the answer to the question of why God created the world as he did is beyond our understanding, because it resides in the mind of God. However, Bacon continued, this does not mean we can't explore the "how" question. In this life we may never know *why* God chose to bring a certain thing to pass, but by careful exploration and experimentation we can discern a great deal about *how* he did it. For example, we may never know why God chose to create this particular universe, but we can discover a great deal about the processes God used to bring it about.

For the most part, the discipline of science took Bacon's advice to heart and has experienced spectacular success as a result. By narrowing the field of study and by holding to relatively modest ambitions (i.e., seeking answers only to the "how" and not the "why"), science has uncovered a wealth of information about the natural world. Scientific progress has exponentially increased our knowledge of the natural world. The application of this knowledge in fields such as medicine has dramatically improved the human condition. For these accomplishments we should commend science and give thanks to God.

Bacon was a devout Christian who believed that studying the world increases our understanding of the works of God. By restricting scientific inquiry to the *how* questions, Bacon was not denying the validity of the *why* questions. Instead, he held that those questions can be answered only by divine revelation.

Bacon believed that if we are going to know the mind of God and think his thoughts after him, then we were going to have to search the Scriptures and come to know his Son, Jesus Christ. Unfortunately, many of the later adherents of the "Baconian Method" came to believe that there is no answer to the "why" question. In their view, science had rendered obsolete any belief in purpose or design. Bacon would have opposed their conclusions completely.

The Concept of a Good World

The Bible teaches that nature has value. In the Genesis 1 creation account, God repeatedly declares that what he has made is "good" (vv. 4, 10, 12, 18, 21, 25) and "very good" (v. 31). The ancient Greeks lacked this conviction. For instance, the Gnostics were a heretical group in the early church who rejected that Jesus has a physical body. Their aberrant views about Christ reflected the Greek worldview that saw the material world as intrinsically evil. The ancient Greeks believed that the world was a prison from which one could only hope to flee. For Christians, the biblical doctrine of creation, along with the incarnation and the coming kingdom of God, demonstrates that the universe has great significance. We live in a world worth saving.

In fact, the very notion of progress is a Christian concept. Since the world has value and God has good plans for it, this means that the world "is going somewhere." The Christian faith teaches that nature has purpose because God created the world for his purposes. The other ancient cultures saw history in cyclic, fatalistic, or deterministic terms. They had no reason to expect improvement or progress.

By contrast, the biblical doctrine of creation is the beginning of a grand narrative that is linear and open to divine activity. In the course of time, God can create something genuinely new. Many concerned about environmental injustice fail to appreciate that the concept of "ought" is a Christian idea. Dissatisfaction with the way things are and the determination to work to make things the way they ought to be is very much a Christian relic in Western culture. In many ways secular notions of progress are attempts to have the kingdom without the King.

Christianity and science are not in conflict. Christianity birthed science. Christianity provided the conceptual worldview, the ethical sanction, and the moral motivation for doing science. We live in a universe created by a good God, and this universe reflects his nature and character (Rom 1:18–20). The universe follows "laws" that scientists can discover. This ability that we have—the ability to comprehend the world and discover the laws that govern it—speaks to the fact that we are created in God's image. We are able to "think God's thoughts after him."

3

How Does God Involve Himself in the World?

In the first two chapters, we examined the ways that Christianity and science have interacted and continue to interact. Now we move to a more theological question: How does God interact with the world? If you were to ask a group of Christians this question, you would likely get a variety of answers. Some might say that each moment of the world's existence is a miracle—a separate creation by God. This view is called "occasionalism," and it understands God to be like an animator who directly designs or creates each scene independently. There are some Christians who hold to occasionalism but not many in comparison to other perspectives.

By contrast, the belief that God created the world but then largely removed himself from its day-to-day operations is called "deism." Under this way of thinking, at the moment of creation God brought the physical world into existence and established a set of properties and relationships (i.e., natural laws) before taking a step back. From this perspective, God acts more like an absentee landlord. Though it was popular among thinkers around 250 years ago (about the time of the American Revolution), deism has since lost much of its luster.

As you can probably tell, occasionalism and deism are opposite viewpoints that represent the extreme ends of the spectrum. Occasionalists would say that each moment is supernatural, while a deist would argue that—other than the initial creation moment—everything in the universe follows natural law. Most Christian theologians and scientists accept something between these extremes—a mediating view if you will. Here we will address one such mediating position called "hypernaturalism."[1] In their book *Hypernaturalism: Integrating the Bible and Science*, Hugh Henry and Daniel J. Dyke argue that God interacts with the world in three ways: naturally, supernaturally, and "hypernaturally."[2] When God works through nature, we typically understand this as God's providence, and when he acts supernaturally, we call this a miracle. To sum it up: positioned between supernaturalism and naturalism is hypernaturalism. What is meant by "hypernatural" can be easily understood once we have a clear grasp of providence and miracle.

---

[1] For a discussion of the various views, see C. John Collins, *The God of Miracles: An Exegetical Examination of God's Action in the World* (Wheaton, IL: Crossway, 2000).

[2] Hugh Henry and Daniel J. Dyke, *Hypernaturalism: Integrating the Bible and Science* (Cincinnati: Mars Hill Center, 2018).

Providence: The Ordinary Way That God Works

The Bible presents Israel's God as the sovereign Creator of the world (Ps 24:1–2). He upholds the universe, comprehensively providing for the needs of all creatures—human and otherwise. Scripture points to the regularities of nature as evidence of his faithfulness (Ps 65:9–13). The psalmist declared, "He causes grass to grow for the livestock and provides crops for man to cultivate. . . . He made the moon to mark the festivals; the sun knows when to set" (Ps 104:14, 19). The prophet Jeremiah also appealed to the routine cycles of the solar system—daily, monthly, and yearly—as evidences of God's steadfast care (Jer 31:35–37). We call this upholding of ordinary processes God's providence.

The New Testament continues the theme of God's faithful, providential care. In the Sermon on the Mount, Jesus spoke about how God provides for us: "Consider the birds of the sky: They don't sow or reap or gather into barns, yet your heavenly Father feeds them. . . . Observe how the wildflowers of the field grow: They don't labor or spin thread. Yet I tell you that not even Solomon in all his splendor was adorned like one of these" (Matt 6:26–29). The ordinary, minute things of life are under God's attentive care, and he works through the ordinary processes to provide for all things.

God's ordinary providence makes science possible, and this fact is often not recognized by even believers. We typically take nature's regularities for granted, not appreciating how mundane routineness profoundly impacts the way we experience the world. It means that we do not live in a magical world in which things inexplicably happen without rhyme or reason. As Henry and Dyke point out, we don't live in a quirky world in which rivers flow downhill one day and then uphill the next.[3]

Historians of science point out that the very fact that we think in terms of natural versus supernatural is a product of the Bible's influence on Western culture.[4] The ancient Near Eastern world in which the Bible originated was a world in which *everything* was understood to be alive and divine. The sun, moon, sky, rivers—literally everything—were understood to be deities. The creation account in Genesis pushed back against all of that. The Bible presents God as creating everything in an orderly, step-by-step manner. It also teaches that the elements of the world—the sky, the moon, and the sun—are not deities. Rather they are mere things made by God for his purposes. The ancient world believed in astrology and searched earnestly for celestial messages. By contrast, Scripture denounces astrology and declares that stars are not magically in control of human destinies (Gen 1:16; Deut 4:19). In this way the first chapter of Genesis "de-deified" nature and led to the natural versus supernatural distinction.

Because the universe follows consistent, regular patterns and relationships, we humans are able to study and identify those patterns and relationships. Science is the careful study of the observable universe. The regularities in nature that scientists discover are called "the laws of nature." Thus, science can be understood to be the study of God's ordinary providence.

---

[3] Henry and Dyke, 25.

[4] See Nancy Pearcey and Charles Thaxton, *The Soul of Science: Christian Faith and Natural Philosophy* (Wheaton, IL: Crossway, 1994).

Miracles: The Extraordinary Ways God Works

Miracles are very, very rare. Miracles were just as unusual in biblical times as they are today. This is one of the reasons Jesus's miracles caused such a stir. Other prophets before him had performed miracles (particularly Moses, Elijah, and Elisha), as did the apostles who followed him. But Jesus performed miracles as a matter of course—something no other prophet ever did. The Bible speaks of him often healing every sick person who came to him. The blind saw, the deaf heard, the lame walked, and lepers suddenly had the skin of newborn babes. Even the dead came back to life. The miracles Jesus performed let the people of his day know that the King of the universe had arrived.

The Bible teaches that miracles always have a purpose. Miracles do not occur simply because believers pray hard enough, say the right incantation, or for some reason convince God to act (even though miracles are often associated with prayer). Christians regularly bring requests to our heavenly Father, but we typically expect him to work through providential means. In fact, Christians who regularly pray often report that their prayers are answered, albeit via the subtle, everyday avenues of life. If God answers in a way that appears to be miraculous, we are (almost) as surprised as nonbelievers.

God does not perform miracles willy-nilly or whimsically. Rather, miracles are "signs and wonders" (Acts 2:22; 14:3; 2 Cor 12:12; Heb 2:4). Miracles are sometimes called "first order activities." This is because they are direct and immediate; that is, there appears to be no mediating element between God and the thing acted upon. Richard Purtill gives a very good, five-part definition of miracles: "A miracle is an event (1) brought about by the power of God that is (2) a temporary (3) exception (4) to the ordinary course of nature (5) for the purpose of showing that God has acted in history."[5] Miracles, then, are not ends in and of themselves but signs that point to a greater truth that God wants us to see.

We should not consider miracles to be "violations of the laws of nature." As we noted in the section before, what we call the laws of nature are our formulations of the regular relationships and properties upheld by God. If he chooses to act in a unique way or in an inexplicable manner, no violation has occurred. God is not bound by the laws of nature; he is above and beyond them.

However, the notion of "violation of the laws of nature" calls attention to an important point. We live in a world of ordinary regularities—of cause and effect—that are predictable enough that we can study these phenomena in a careful, scientific manner. One identifying trait of a miracle is that it disrupts the discernible chain of cause and effect. Consider the moment that a miracle occurs. There is nothing in the prior moment's state of affairs that indicated a miracle was going to happen in the next moment. One moment the leper's skin was diseased; the next moment his skin is healed. The same is true of the blind suddenly seeing or the corpse suddenly breathing. A miracle is an arresting, disjointed occurrence.

Miracles, by definition, cannot be explained scientifically. There is nothing regular, persistent, or predictable about them.

---

[5] Richard Purtill, "Defining Miracles," in *In Defense of Miracles: A Comprehensive Case for God's Action in History*, ed. Douglas Geivett and Gary Habermas (Downers Grove, IL: IVP, 1997), 72.

They are rare, extraordinary, and awe-inspiring; and as signs and wonders, they happen for a reason. The Bible teaches that when Jesus turned the water into wine, walked on the water, and other similar miracles, these events were beacons directing his disciples to the truth about Jesus and his work. Providence can be studied by science; miracles cannot.

Hypernatural Events: The Way God Occasionally Works

There is much more that we could say about providence and miracles, but we have said enough to have a good working concept of both. Having surveyed the ways that God works naturally and supernaturally in the world, we are now able to turn our attention to God's hypernatural actions.

Hypernaturalism Defined

So what are hypernatural events? Henry and Dyke define *hypernaturalism* thus: "Hypernaturalism is defined as the extraordinary use of natural law by the God described in the Bible. When God acts hypernaturally, He employs natural law and natural phenomena in an extraordinary way to bring about His will."[6] A hypernatural event is the point at which providence and miracles intersect. The event is providential in the sense that it uses natural law and natural mechanisms, but it is miraculous in the sense that its results go beyond what can be accounted for naturally.

---

[6] Henry and Dyke, *Hypernaturalism*, 25.

Biblical Examples of Hypernatural Events

Hypernaturalism is an admittedly challenging concept, but it is in line with the teaching of Scripture. The Bible records a remarkable number of occasions in which it can be said that God worked hypernaturally. These occasions can be categorized in at least four ways.

Extraordinarily Fortuitous Natural Events

The first type to consider are extraordinarily fortuitous natural events. These are rare occurrences that happen in the natural world that seem almost too good to be true. These events defy logical explanation and can only be understood as instances of divine intervention.

The Bible gives several examples. Matthew 17 gives the remarkable account of how Jesus provided the money to pay the temple tax for Simon Peter and himself. When Jesus sent Peter fishing, Jesus told Peter that when he checked the mouth of the first fish he caught, he would find a gold coin that he could use to pay the temple tax. Note how many "natural" elements there are in this event. Fish, coins, and the act of going fishing are all natural things. Perhaps catching a fish that already has something in its mouth is something that might happen occasionally. But when the fish has money in its mouth, exactly the amount Peter needed and exactly as Jesus predicted, then something extraordinary is going on. This is not a miracle in the precise, supernatural sense, but it defies natural explanation. This is something in between—a hypernatural event.

Daniel 6 provides another example of hypernaturalism. When Daniel was thrown into the lions' den, God closed the lions' mouths (Dan 6:22–24). The text points out that when Daniel's adversaries were subsequently thrown in, they were immediately eaten.

Again, consider Jesus calming the storm on the Sea of Galilee (Mark 4:35–41). He rebuked the wind and waves as if they were sentient beings. In this case, Jesus spoke to the natural order, and it responded obediently. The event was both providential and miraculous because Jesus interacted with natural law in an extraordinary way. The Bible says that the disciples thought they were scared by the storm but that they were even more scared by the immediate calming of the storm. Mark 4:41 observes that when the disciples paused to consider who was in the boat with them, they became truly alarmed. The hypernatural event got the message across.

God's Use of Secondary Means

The book of Exodus gives numerous examples of God acting directly and immediately. The ten plagues were primarily brought about by God miraculously. However, the narrative also recounts instances when God worked indirectly. At times the Lord used secondary, natural means to accomplish the task at hand. In Exodus 14, God parted the sea so that Israel could escape Pharaoh's army. But the text says that "the Lord drove the sea back with a powerful east wind" (v. 21). This is an illustration of a hypernatural, providential miracle. God used natural means to bring about his will. The wind was not supernatural in the strict sense, nor was it providential in the narrow sense. It was providence and miracle all at once, a hypernatural event.

Another fascinating example is provided by Scripture and then elaborated further by science. Genesis 19 tells how God destroyed Sodom and Gomorrah by raining fire from the sky. It also recounts how Abraham's nephew, Lot, barely escaped with his life but his wife did not. When she turned around to look back, she "became a pillar of salt" (v. 26). Archaeologists have excavated the Dead Sea area where the cities were. They have found compelling evidence that, at about the time recounted in Genesis 19, the entire region was immediately vaporized by a comet or meteorite that exploded in the sky above.[7] The blast appears to have been 1,000 times greater than the Hiroshima atomic bomb. Interestingly, the reports state that the fiery explosion blasted large quantities of saline deposits into the air and that anyone unfortunate enough to be watching nearby would have been immediately encrusted in salt (Gen 19:26).

Prophetic Knowledge of Future Events

One trait that characterized the prophets of the Bible was their ability to foretell events. The events often were not miraculous in themselves. Many times, the prophecies were forecasts of births, deaths, victories or defeats in battles, and kings ascending or losing power—all mundane, natural occurrences. It was the prophets' ability to accurately predict an event that was remarkable. In addition to accuracy, the prophets often

---

[7] Livia Gershon, "Ancient City's Destruction by Exploding Space Rock May Have Inspired Biblical Story of Sodom," https://www.smithsonianmag.com/smart-news/destruction-of-city-by-space-rock-may-have-inspired-biblical-story-of-sodom-180978734/.

predicted precise details. In 1 Kings 21 the prophet Elijah not only predicted the way in which wicked Queen Jezebel would die, but he also added that her body would be consumed by wild dogs (v. 23). Second Kings 9 records how Elijah's prophecy was fulfilled completely, including the gruesome detail of what happened to her corpse. The overthrow and execution of evil rulers occur often in history. The hypernatural aspects were the accuracy and precision of the prophet's prophecy.

Second Kings 7 recounts how the city of Samaria was experiencing famine because it was surrounded by an invading army. The prophet Elisha predicted an imminent end of the siege and a sudden windfall of food. When one of the king's bureaucrats scoffed, Elisha told him, "You will in fact see it with your own eyes, but you won't eat any of it" (v. 2). The next day it was discovered that the enemy had left the night before in a panic, leaving behind stockpiles of supplies. As the inhabitants of the city stampeded to gather the food, they trampled to death the bureaucrat. Elisha's prophecy was fulfilled to the letter.

The Bible provides example after example. Isaiah predicted the rise of Cyrus over two centuries before his birth (Isa 44:28–45:4). In Daniel 2, the prophet foretold a succession of four world empires that would arise and fall in subsequent centuries. In Ezekiel 26, the prophet Ezekiel predicted the fall of Tyre, and it was fulfilled in detail to the exact day (Ezek 29:17–20). The extraordinary ability of the prophets to predict world events fits well with the definition of hypernatural.

God's Exercise of Special Providence

In addition to extremely fortuitous occurrences, the use of secondary means, and fulfilled prophecies, Scripture provides numerous examples of God acting hypernaturally by subtly yet meticulously controlling events. Some examples would be the roll of the dice (Prov 16:33), the decisions made by rulers (Prov 21:1), and human actions both good and bad (Gen 50:20). God manages to perfectly accomplish his will in such a way that humans still act freely and thus are accountable. The Bible does not explain how God is able to do this. Throughout the history of the church, theologians have argued with each other about this mystery, and it is safe to predict that those arguments will continue until the end of the age.

God hypernaturally works through what would otherwise be ordinary natural occurrences—the wind blowing from a certain direction, food being left behind by an army fleeing in haste, a young woman giving birth—to bring about his plan and purposes.

Providence or Miracle?

So are hypernatural events examples of providence, or are they miracles? It is easy to see why the language of miracle would be used. Henry and Dyke themselves categorize hypernatural occurrences as a special subset of miracles. They explain, "Acknowledgement of the phenomenon of hypernaturalism seems important in the 21st century because—with the advance of science—nonbelievers are claiming that many of God's miracles are actually natural occurrences."[8] Nonbelievers see hypernatural events—God doing the impossible by means of his control over the forces of nature—as natural miracles.

[8] Henry and Dyke, *Hypernaturalism*, 12.

However, the argument for viewing hypernatural events as providential occurrences is also strong. Theologians generally break down providence into two categories: general providence and special providence. General providence is God's overall care of the entire created order. It is this type of providence that this chapter has been discussing. Special providence refers to the particular care God shows to his people—Israel in the Old Testament and the church in the New Testament. Hypernaturalism can be understood to be a very, very special type of special providence.

Scientific Examples of Hypernatural Events

Remarkably, science itself has provided some of the most compelling examples of hypernatural events. In the next few chapters, we will examine the best known examples: the big bang, the fine-tuning argument, the Rare Earth hypothesis, the origin of life enigma, and others. These are examples about which there is general scientific agreement. There is broad consensus among scientists about each of the findings we will examine. Paradoxically, there is no broad scientific agreement as to why these things exist or how they could have happened. Natural explanations seem to fall short. In each case the only explanation that fits all the facts and evidence is providential, in other words, a hypernatural explanation.

Hypernaturalism has one basic goal: to demonstrate that providence, not simply chance or necessity, is the driving force behind all of creation. This includes both natural and supernatural events. As humans we are limited in our ability to comprehend God's providential activity within his created order.

This activity often appears miraculous to us because it goes beyond what we would expect. That is hypernaturalism: providence beyond what we would expect. It is providence beyond providence, providential activity that goes beyond natural laws and defies our limited understanding of God's providential activity. In other words, it is God's providential activity in natural history that appears to be miraculous.

As previously stated, this book takes an *arguendo* approach. Our engagement with the majority opinions of the scientific community does not mean that we automatically agree with those conclusions. Instead, we will assume those conclusions to be true in order to explore the implications of those findings. This approach allows us to move beyond naturalism and supernaturalism to an even bigger view of God's providential activity that extends across all of creation—hypernaturalism. Hypernaturalism reminds us that our God is both provident and miraculous.

4

Creation and the Big Bang

The Bible begins with ten words that encompass everything: "In the beginning God created the heavens and the earth" (Gen 1:1). God, without the use of preexisting materials, brought the world into existence by his sovereign power, for his own good will and pleasure. The universe, which initially was not, suddenly was. Scripture teaches *creatio ex nihilo*—creation out of nothing. Science also teaches a version of *creatio ex nihilo*—the big bang theory. In his *Origin Story: A Big History of Everything*, David Christian pithily explains, "We don't know what Goldilocks conditions allowed a universe to emerge, and we still can't explain it any better than novelist Terry Pratchett did when he wrote, 'The current state of knowledge can be summarized thus: In the beginning, there was nothing, which exploded.'"[1]

Fewer than 100 years ago a Roman Catholic priest named Georges Lemaitre (1894–1966) first proposed the big bang

[1] David Christian, *Origin Story: A Big History of Everything* (New York: Little, Brown, and Spark, 2018), 20.

theory. Initially many in the scientific community resisted the hypothesis, and they did so for explicitly anti-religious reasons. The prevailing theory at the time was that the universe had always existed, pretty much in the same state as we see it now. Later this view was developed into the "steady state" model. A steady state universe would not need a Creator because it never would have been created. The big bang theory, by contrast, held that the universe had a beginning, and this implied that there was a Beginner.

The Big Bang Theory

The big bang theory states that the universe was born from an incredibly dense and hot singularity, which then rapidly expanded. The big bang event occurred around 14 billion years ago, and it appears that the universe has been expanding ever since. This initial expansion caused the formation of matter and energy, as well as space-time itself.

What was happening prior to the big bang? The answer is that there is no "prior" to the big bang. This is because time itself was created at that moment. Honestly, no human can really grasp the notion of a timeless reality *before* the big bang. However, the concept is not new. Augustine had a curt reply to anyone who dared to ask what God was doing before he created the world. "He was preparing hell . . . for those who pry into such mysteries."[2] Augustine argued that the question had no meaning—if time is an element of creation, then there was no

---

[2] Aurelius Augustine, *Confessions*, 11.12.14, trans. J. G. Pilkington, in *Nicene and Post-Nicene Fathers*, vol. 1, ed. Philip Schaff (Buffalo, NY: Christian Literature, 1887). Revised and edited for New Advent by Kevin Knight, http://www.newadvent.org/fathers/110111.htm.

"before" the events of Gen 1:1. In most models, the universe started out as a point smaller than an atom. Using the laws of physics, scientists can "rewind the video" to within 10^{-43} of a second after the universe began. At this point the laws of physics (as we currently know them) break down. What happened before this moment and what happened at the initial moment are beyond the reach of science.[3]

At the moment of the big bang, all matter was condensed into a hot and extremely dense state with temperatures reaching up to 10^{32}K (10 billion degrees Celsius). Scientists believe that immediately after its beginning, the expansion of the space-time fabric of the universe caused everything to cool rapidly. The big bang expansion process generated radiation that spread across the universe in waves called cosmic microwave background radiation (CMBR). This CMBR is detectable today and provides strong evidence for the big bang theory.

---

[3] There is also the "Inflationary Model" of the big bang hypothesis. Astrophysicist and apologist Jeff Zweerink explains how the inflationary model differs from the standard model: "In most inflationary big bang models, the scenario differs in these ways: 1. Some pre-existing 'space' continually undergoes inflation. 2. Our universe begins when inflation stops in some region of this 'space.' 3. If viewed from outside our universe, this bubble region where inflation ceased grows larger as time progresses. The boundary between the inflating region outside the bubble and the non-inflating region inside the bubble represents the big bang. Those inside the bubble cannot see out; those outside the bubble cannot see in. 4. The region inside the bubble cools down, eventually emitting the cosmic microwave background radiation, forming stars and galaxies. Almost 14 billion years later, human beings arrive on planet Earth." See Jeff Zweerink, "Multiverse Musings—Does It Jive with the Big Bang?," Reasons to Believe, October 7, 2009, https://reasons.org/explore/publications/articles/multiverse-musings-does-it-jive-with-the-big-bang.

As the universe continued to expand and cool, it reached temperatures where hydrogen could fuse to form helium. These two elements would become essential for the creation of stars later in the history of the universe. Moreover, as time progressed, gravity began to cause enormous amounts of gas to collect and collapse, forming stars around 100 million years after the big bang. This process eventually led to galaxies with their own stellar populations being formed over time due to gravitational forces pulling together even more interstellar material at larger scales than before. By 300 million years after the big bang, these new galaxies were already forming structures—such as arms containing gas, dust, and other luminous matter spread across vast distances.

Nowadays it is believed that the mysterious forces that initiated the big bang continue to affect our universe. For example, astronomers measure something called "dark energy," which at this point is unknown, is pushing against gravity's pull and is, in fact, causing the universe's expansion to accelerate. Dark energy has many similarities to the stuff that caused inflation in the earliest moments of our universe. As scientists investigate dark energy and understand the process of inflation more, the evidence that everything had a beginning grows stronger and stronger.[4] Science has discovered much over the past century, but clearly there is much yet to learn. But one thing appears to be settled: the cosmos is not eternal. It has a finite age.

---

[4] It's important to note that inflationary models still require a beginning. See Arvind Borde, Alan Guth, and Alexander Vilenkin, "Inflationary Spacetimes Are Incomplete in Past Directions," *Physical Review Letters* 90, no. 15 (April 2003), https://doi.org/10.1103/PhysRevLett.90.151301.

Creation Versus Eternalism

In the days of the early church, the debate was not about the age of the earth or about evolution versus creation. The debate was about whether or not the world was ever created at all.

The Ancient Belief in Eternalism

The predominant view among Greco-Roman philosophers was that the cosmos was eternal. They rejected the notion of *creatio ex nihilo* ("creation out of nothing"), arguing instead that *ex nihilo nihil fit* ("out of nothing comes nothing"). Aristotle declared, "We ourselves are in agreement with them in holding that nothing can be said without qualification to come from what is not."[5] In his book *On the Eternity of the World*, the neo-Platonic philosopher Proclus (AD 410–85) gave eighteen arguments why the universe had always existed.

The early Christian theologians were adamant in their affirmation of *creatio ex nihilo*. Even though they were intellectually swimming against the tide, they were willing to do so because they understood what was at stake. If the world was just as eternal as God, then it would not and could not be under his sovereign control. It would also mean that the evil and sin currently in the world was "baked in," that is, a feature that was always part of the world; thus, there was no real hope of redemption and transformation.

---

[5] Aristotle, *Physics*, 1.8.191b13, in *The Complete Works of Aristotle: The Revised Oxford Translation*, vol. 1, ed. Jonathan Barnes (Princeton, NJ: Princeton University Press, 1991), 16, https://sites.unimi.it/zucchi/NuoviFile/Barnes%20%20-%20Physics.pdf.

Early heretical groups, such as the Manichees, accepted this fatalistic outlook. The early church fathers defended the biblical doctrine of creation because they realized that it was foundational for a proper understanding of salvation. The Son of God, Creator of heaven and earth, took on flesh to die for our sins and save the world. Eventually, through the writings of Christian thinkers such Tertullian, Irenaeus, and Augustine, *creatio ex nihilo* won the day. Belief that the universe was created and had a beginning in time predominated throughout the medieval era.

The Return of Eternalism

The Scientific Revolution of the sixteenth and seventeenth centuries marked a pivotal point in human history. It witnessed monumental advancements in scientific thought and methodology, with many key figures emerging from this period. At the forefront was Nicolaus Copernicus (1473–1543), who proposed his heliocentric model of the solar system in 1543. This model was in stark contrast to the geocentric model favored by Ptolemy, which had been the accepted view for centuries. Johannes Kepler (1571–1630) built on Copernicus's work by demonstrating that the planets move in an ellipse instead of a circle.

No scientist during this time was more influential than Sir Isaac Newton (1642–1727). Newton formulated the laws of gravity that comprehensively described planetary motion. Gravity, Newton explained, was a force that operated on all objects in the universe. The larger an object is, the greater its gravitational pull. The greater the distance between two objects, the lesser the attraction. Newton invented a whole new field of mathematics, calculus, in order to precisely work out the laws of motion and the laws of gravity.

Newton's laws of gravity created one obvious problem that was quickly noted. Universal gravitation means that everything in the universe is pulling everything else toward it. Why wasn't there a big, universal crunch? Newton responded by theorizing that the cosmos was infinite in size; thus, the gravitational pull was equal from every direction and canceled each other out. However, if the universe is infinite, that implies it is also eternal. Thus, eternalism returned as the prevailing view. Newton himself was a fervent, albeit heterodox, Christian. However this was the time that would come to be known as the Enlightenment. The reasons for the Enlightenment are complex and varied, and most have little to do with the matter at hand. Many during this era rejected orthodox Christianity in favor of a benign deism or skepticism. They saw Newton's model as grounds for rejecting the biblical doctrine of creation in favor of an eternal, steady state universe. The Newtonian steady state version of eternalism served as the basis for classical physics until the early twentieth century.

Theoretical physicist Simon Singh explains why scientists found eternalism attractive: "An eternal universe seemed to strike a chord with the scientific community, because the theory had a certain elegance, simplicity and completeness. If the universe has existed for eternity, then there was no need to explain how it was created, when it was created, why it was created or Who created it. Scientists were particularly proud that they had developed a theory of the universe that no longer relied on invoking God."[6]

---

[6] Simon Singh, quoted in Stephen Meyer, *Return of the God Hypothesis: Three Scientific Discoveries that Reveal the Mind behind the Universe* (New York: HarperOne, 2021), 73.

Eternalism played a crucial role in the arguments made for Darwinism by its early advocates.[7] Darwinists conceded that the odds of something as complex as living beings coming about by random chance were extremely low, even minuscule. However, if the cosmos is eternal, then it does not matter how unlikely an event may be. Given an infinite amount of time, if an event has any possibility of happening at all—no matter how remote—then inevitably it will happen. In an everlasting universe it does not matter how many trillions of years it might take. Eventually every possible scenario will get its day. We are here, so obviously our existence is possible. Therefore, concluded the Darwinists, as absurdly improbable as it is, an eternal and infinite universe renders our evolution inevitable.

Eternalism, by its very nature, is fatalistic. By the end of the nineteenth century, scientists and philosophers were grappling with the implications of an eternal cosmos. In Germany, Ernst Haeckel (1834–1919) and Friedrich Nietzsche (1844–1900) argued that eternalism meant the death of God, human freedom, and any sense of morality. Perhaps Nietzsche saw most clearly where eternalism led. He argued for what he called "the eternal recurrence theorem." This theorem argues that an infinite universe does not just render our improbable existence inevitable; it also means that we have occurred again and again in the past and that we will recur in the future *ad infinitum*. We are caught in an endless loop. Life has no purpose, nor can it have any. Nietzsche embraced nihilism, the view that "life leads to nothing" and that existence is "useless, empty, and

---

[7] These three paragraphs are dependent on my *40 Questions about Creation and Evolution* (Grand Rapids, MI: Kregel, 2010), 185–87.

absurd."[8] However, discoveries and advances in physics and astronomy at the beginning of the next century would overturn both steady-state cosmology and eternalism.

The Rise of the Big Bang Theory

Not long after Nietzsche died, Albert Einstein (1879–1955) published his general theory of relativity (in 1916), and it upended classical Newtonian physics. It was an incredibly revolutionary idea that changed the way we think about physics and space-time. Einstein proposed that gravity is not a force in itself but rather is an effect caused by the warping and bending of space-time due to objects with mass. However, since all matter has this space-bending property, his theory seemed to imply that everything in the universe would congeal or bunch up together. And since space itself is being bent by mass, Newton's theory of infinite space no longer provided a solution. Mathematical attempts to reconcile an eternal, steady universe with Einstein's theory required adding arbitrary constants that had little justification.

---

[8] "In infinity, at some moment or other, every possible combination must once have been realized; not only this, but it must once have been realized an infinite number of times. . . . If all possible combinations and relations of forces had not already been exhausted, then an infinity would not yet lie behind us. Now since infinite time must be assumed, no fresh possibility can exist and everything must have appeared already, and moreover an infinite number of times." Friedrich Nietzsche, quoted in Frank J. Tipler, *The Physics of Immortality: Modern Cosmology, God and the Resurrection of the Dead* (New York: Doubleday, 1994), 74–103.

About this time astronomer Edwin Hubble (1899–1953) noticed that, according to the evidence he was collecting, all galaxies in the universe are doing something odd. They are all moving away from each other. As mentioned before, Georges Lemaitre (who was both a physicist and a priest) had already mathematically extrapolated this evidence backward. He proposed that the reason everything is moving away from each other is because originally there was a tremendous explosion that brought everything into existence. Lemaitre likened the universe at this initial moment to a "cosmic egg" or a "primordial atom."[9] Because of his proposal, Lemaitre is considered to be the father of the theory of the big bang.

Einstein had already tried to avoid the indications that the cosmos had a beginning, and he had inserted a "cosmological constant" into his equations in order to retain the idea of a static universe. When he met Lemaitre in 1925, Einstein told him, "Your calculations are correct, but your physics is abominable." Einstein later explained that he opposed the big bang hypothesis because it was "inspired by the Christian dogma of creation, and totally unjustified from the physical point of view."[10] Eventually he admitted that his opposition to Lemaitre was wrong and that his subsequent hypothesis of a cosmological constant was one of the biggest mistakes of his career.

Many other physicists and astronomers joined him in his opposition to the universe having a beginning. In his book, *God and the Astronomers*, Robert Jastrow demonstrates that much of the hostility came from an anti-religious bias. In 1931,

---

[9] Christian, *Origin Story*, 21.

[10] Meyer, *Return of the God Hypothesis*, 145.

astronomer Arthur Eddington flatly stated, "The notion of a beginning is repugnant to me."[11]

No one opposed the idea of the universe having a beginning more than astronomer Sir Fred Hoyle (1915–2001). To make fun of the theory he coined the term "big bang," and the expression stuck. In 1948, Hoyle proposed an alternative to the big bang, called the "steady state theory." This theory states that the universe is eternal, with matter being continuously created to keep the universe always looking the same. In other words, as the fabric of space-time expands to ever-increasing sizes (and drags matter with it), new matter is simultaneously created to maintain a constant average density throughout the entire universe.

However, by the 1960s the evidence seemed to be more and more in favor of the big bang theory. As noted earlier, the theory predicted that the entire universe should give evidence of being bathed in faint, cosmic background microwave radiation (CMBR). In 1965 radio astronomers Arno Penzias and Robert Wilson accidentally discovered CMBR. By the 1980s the CMBR had been carefully mapped, and its features were exactly as the big bang theory predicted. Numerous other supporting evidence accumulated, so by the end of the twentieth century, the big bang theory was the reigning paradigm in the scientific community. Even Hoyle conceded that the steady state theory was dead. Jastrow sums up the situation with a quote that has become famous: "For the scientist who has lived by his faith in the power of reason, the story ends like a bad

---

[11] Robert Jastrow, *God and the Astronomers* (New York: W. W. Norton, 1992), 102.

dream. He has scaled the mountains of ignorance; he is about to conquer the highest peak; as he pulls himself over the final rock, he is greeted by a band of theologians who have been sitting there for centuries."[12]

The Theological Implications of the Big Bang

The medieval theologian Thomas Aquinas (1225–74) was noted for his arguments for the existence of God. One of his arguments, the cosmological argument, is built on the premise that the universe had a beginning. It goes like this: (1) Whatever begins to exist must have a cause. (2) The universe began to exist. (3) Therefore, the universe must have had a Cause. This cause must be greater than the universe it brought about. It must be both prior to and outside of the universe it produced, and it must have both the power and the wisdom to produce it. Aquinas concluded we have a name that we call this Cause—God. Aquinas's logic is compelling.

There have been several attempts to avoid the obvious theological implications of the big bang. Some have suggested an infinite regress of universes, one causing another, of which our universe is the latest iteration. However, there is nothing to indicate that our universe will produce another one in the future. Others have posited the theory that the universe might be oscillating—that it endlessly goes through cycles of expansion and contraction. We just happen to be currently in a cycle of expansion. But in 2003, cosmologists demonstrated that our

[12] Jastrow, 105–6.

universe must have had an absolute beginning, so the oscillating universe model has been abandoned.[13]

Lately some have suggested that the big bang was the product of a quantum fluctuation. This theory proposes that in the moments before the big bang, space and time were part of a single unified state that contained all of the energy and matter that would form into the universe. The big bang was then triggered by a random quantum fluctuation in this state, which caused space and time to expand outward from the universe we know today. However, the second law of thermodynamics shows that entropy, the level of disorder, is constantly increasing. This means that at the moment of the big bang, the level of order must have been billions and billions of time greater than it is now. Thus, it is more likely that a quantum fluctuation would bring the universe instantly into existence as it is now than that a quantum fluctuation would create the universe as it was at the time of the big bang. This realization has caused most cosmologists to dismiss the quantum fluctuation model as too implausible.[14]

Caltech astronomer Allan Sandage (1926–2010) was one of the premier cosmologists of the twentieth century. A student of Edwin Hubble, he further refined Hubble's research after Hubble died in 1953. He was well-known as an agnostic who adhered to a materialist understanding of the universe. In 1985,

---

[13] Although recently some scientists have proposed a "cyclical model." See Jeff Zweerink, "Multiverse Musings: Is It Testable?," Reasons to Believe, November 26, 2013, https://reasons.org/explore/publications/articles/multiverse-musings-is-it-testable.

[14] Roger Penrose, *The Emperor's New Mind: Concerning Computers, Minds, and the Laws of Physics* (New York: Penguin Books, 1991), 339–45.

at a conference on the big bang, Sandage shocked the audience by announcing his religious conversion.[15] He explained how he had come to view the big bang as a "creation event":

> Here is evidence for what can only be described as a supernatural event. There is no way that this could have been predicted within the realm of physics as we know it. . . . Science, until recently, has concerned itself not with primary causes but, essentially, with secondary causes. What has happened in the last fifty years is a remarkable event within astronomy and astrophysics. By looking up at the sky, some astronomers have come to the belief that there is evidence for a "creation event."[16]

Though Sandage does not use the language of hypernaturalism to describe the big bang, in effect what he was saying is that the big bang was a hypernatural event.

The big bang theory implies that there is a Cause greater than the universe—something outside our world as we know it caused this big bang to occur. It also demonstrates that the universe is contingent and not self-originating, thus it further corroborates Aquinas's cosmological argument. Finally, the big bang theory shows us that there are limits to scientific inquiry. While science can help us to understand the world brought forth by the big bang, it cannot tell us how this momentous event happened or what existed "prior" to the big bang. The big bang was a hypernatural event, and while it does not provide definitive proof of God's existence, it does fit remarkably well with the biblical doctrine of *creatio ex nihilo*.

---

[15] Meyer, *Return of the God Hypothesis*, 166–67.

[16] Meyer, 166–67.

5

The Fine-Tuning of the Universe

Would you like to win the lottery? Over the past sixty years, state lotteries have become a big business. Today over forty-five states offer lotteries, with many states pooling their resources to become nationwide lotteries with enormous payouts—sometimes over a billion dollars. What if it was discovered that, through the years, all the lottery jackpots were won by a single person? Suppose it was further revealed that that person used aliases to keep it from becoming known that all the jackpots had only one winner. Not only did that one person win every jackpot, but he won every time he played. Lotteries that had no jackpot winner for a particular drawing were the times he didn't play. The odds of winning a lottery jackpot are about 1 in 300 million, but of the hundreds of jackpots claimed over the decades, this one fellow won them all. We wouldn't wonder if something was fishy. We would know the system was rigged.

It turns out that we, the inhabitants of earth, are that lucky fellow—metaphorically speaking. We live in a universe that, for life to exist, had to have scores and scores of variables turn out to be just right. We have repeatedly won the cosmic jackpot. Scientists call this phenomenon the "fine-tuning" of the universe.

What Is Fine-Tuning?

Beginning in the latter half of the twentieth century, scientists began noticing something interesting. Evidence was accumulating that indicated the universe was very, very carefully constructed. Four implications were noted. First, the big bang hypothesis implies that the universe is fine-tuned. Through the big bang, all of space, time, matter, and energy were birthed from a singular event. The initial conditions of this moment had to have been calibrated to a level that is humanly incomprehensible. Our universe, from the smallest particle to the grandest galaxy, is a masterpiece of precision, a symphony orchestrated with such exactitude that it defies our ability to grasp. A delicate balance governs our existence. It is no exaggeration to say that the universe has been formulated with a level of calibration that is quite literally astronomical.

Second, the science behind the fine-tuning argument is well established. The idea of a fine-tuned universe is not a fringe belief but a well-established scientific observation, supported by thinkers such as renowned theoretical physicist Stephen Hawking (1942–2018) and several Nobel Prize winners, including Roger Penrose and Frank Wilczek. The hypothesis is not the product of the musings of poets, theologians, or philosophers. Astrophysicist Hugh Ross reports that over fifty scientists, many unattached to spiritual beliefs, have published books on the subject.[1]

---

[1] Hugh Ross, "How Does Fine-Tuning Make the Case for Nature's Designer?" in *The Comprehensive Guide to Science and Faith:*

Third, we live in a "Goldilocks universe." What if the universe was slightly different from what it actually is? The answer, surprising as it may seem, is that we would not exist. We reside in what many call a "Goldilocks universe," though the conditions are beyond being "just right." Our cosmos is more than "not too hot, not too cold." To change metaphors, the conditions cannot be described as merely on a razor's edge. It's more as if over 100 razors—edge upon edge—were balanced one upon another.

Fourth, the evidence of fine-tuning leads many scientists to embrace the "anthropic principle." Many believing scientists argue that the extremely precise calibration of the universe gives evidence that an Intelligence planned it with purpose and care—hence the name "the fine-tuning argument." Our mathematically elegant universe seems to be specially crafted, a masterpiece of exactitude. Because the universe appears to be precisely designed for human life, the fine-tuning argument is also often called the "anthropic principle."

Fine-Tuning's Greatest Hits

Cosmology and astrophysics provide us with numerous examples of fine-tuning. New evidence is routinely being discovered. Reasons to Believe, an apologetics ministry founded by astrophysicist Hugh Ross, has a website that collects these examples. So far, the compendium lists over 140 examples.[2]

Exploring Ultimate Questions about Life and the Cosmos, ed. William Dembski, Casey Luskin, and Joseph Holden (Eugene, OR: Harvest House, 2021), 229–37.

[2] https://storage.googleapis.com/reasons-prod/files/compendium/compendium_part1.pdf. No longer accessible.

Many of the books that address fine-tuning devote hundreds upon hundreds of pages to presenting and explaining the numerous examples. Reading the barrage of scientific facts can give the reader the sensation of being pummeled to death by ping-pong balls. Since going into such detail is beyond the scope of this primer, let's briefly look at four of the better known and striking examples.[3] First, the relationships among the constants of nature must be exactly what they are to an amazing level of precision. In his book *God's Undertaker: Has Science Buried God?* Oxford mathematician John Lennox discusses the four essential forces in the universe: the strong-nuclear force, the weak-nuclear force, the electromagnetic force, and gravity. He points out that a minor alteration in the ratio of the strong-nuclear force to the electromagnetic force, by just one part in 10^{16}, would make star formation impossible, eliminating the existence of something like our sun. Similarly, a change in the ratio of the electromagnetic force to the gravitational force by one part in 10^{40} would result in the formation of only very small or very large stars, and once again, a star resembling our sun wouldn't be able to exist.[4]

Second, the rate of the expansion of the universe is calibrated with remarkable exactitude. Stephen Hawking pointed out that the universe's expansion was in delicate balance. According to the standard big bang theory, if the expansion had been reduced by a mere one part in 10^{10}, the universe would

---

[3] The following examples are adapted from Kenneth Keathley and Mark Rooker, *40 Questions on Creation and Evolution* (Grand Rapids, MI: Kregel, 2014).

[4] John C. Lennox, *God's Undertaker: Has Science Buried God?* (Oxford: Lion, 2007), 69.

have collapsed rapidly; and of course, no life would have been possible. Conversely, if the expansion had been greater by the same fraction, our universe would now be virtually devoid of matter, essentially empty.

Third, the critically precise balance between protons, electrons, and neutrons. These are, of course, the foundational components of molecules. Physicists have found that an incredibly precise ratio between these particles is essential for the existence of stars and planets. A slight deviation in the number of electrons compared to protons would have caused electromagnetic forces to overwhelm gravitational forces, making the formation of stars and planets impossible. How precise does this balance need to be? The level of exactness is staggering. Ross reveals that the number of electrons must match the number of protons to one part in 10^{37}, an astonishing level of accuracy.[5]

All these examples involve numbers expressed in exponential form, such as 10^{37}. To grasp how colossal 10^{37} is, it's worth acknowledging that it's practically beyond human comprehension. Such an astronomical number often becomes meaningless in our everyday understanding. Ross attempts to put the 1 in 10^{37} odds into perspective with a vivid illustration. Picture the entire United States blanketed with dimes, stacked all the way to the moon. Now, imagine a billion piles of these dimes, each of the same vast size. Within this inconceivable number of coins, only one dime is marked with red paint. Then think of the nearly impossible task of being blindfolded and having to pick

[5] Hugh Ross, *The Creator and the Cosmos: How the Latest Discoveries Reveal God* (Covina, CA: RTB, 2018), 109.

that single red dime from all those coins with just one attempt. When thinking of 1 in 10^{37}, that's the scope of the odds.[6]

Fourth, the universe's precision goes even further, making previous examples seem almost trivial in comparison. Stephen Hawking found that the expansion rate of the universe must be accurate to one part in 10^{55}. Any faster, and there would be no stars, galaxies, or planets; any slower, and the universe would become a massive black hole.[7] Roger Penrose, a collaborator with Hawking on initial black hole research, has shown that the entropy of the universe is precise to one part in $10^{(10)123}$. It's essential to recognize that this number is so enormous that it vastly surpasses the total count of atoms in the universe. The number has so many zeros that it's nearly humanly impossible to write it in standard notation. Penrose states, "I cannot even recall seeing anything else in physics whose accuracy is known to approach, even remotely, a figure like one part in $10^{(10)123}$."[8] Dozens upon dozens of similar examples could be provided, but I think you get the idea. We live in an unimaginably special universe.

Many Astronomers and Physicists Have Begun to Sound Like Theologians

Where do scientists end up when they contemplate such evidence for fine-tuning? Not surprisingly, they arrive at

---

[6] Ross, 109.

[7] Ross, 110.

[8] Cited by William Lane Craig, "Design and the Anthropic Fine-Tuning of the Universe," in *God and Design: The Teleological Argument and Modern Science*, ed. Neil A. Manson (New York: Routledge, 2003), 157.

metaphysics. One of the earliest to write about fine-tuning phenomena was noted astronomer Sir Fred Hoyle (1915–2001). He declared:

> Would you not say to yourself . . . Some supercalculating intellect must have designed the properties of the carbon atom, otherwise the chance of my finding such an atom through the blind forces of nature would be utterly minuscule[?] Of course you would. . . . You would conclude that the carbon atom is a fix. . . .
>
> A common sense interpretation of the facts suggests that a superintellect has monkeyed with physics, as well as with chemistry and biology, and that there are no blind forces worth speaking about in nature. The numbers one calculates from the facts seem to me so overwhelming as to put this conclusion almost beyond question.[9]

Hoyle acknowledged that the discovery of fine-tuning profoundly shook his atheism. Astronomer George Greenstein comes to a similar conclusion as Hoyle: "As we survey all the evidence, the thought insistently arises that some supernatural agency—or, rather, Agency—must be involved. Is it possible that suddenly, without intending to, we have stumbled upon scientific proof of the existence of a Supreme Being? Was it God who stepped in and so providentially crafted the cosmos for our benefit?"[10] Physicist Paul Davies observes,

---

[9] Sir Fred Hoyle, "The Universe: Past and Present Reflections," *Engineering and Science* (November 1981): 12, https://calteches.library.caltech.edu/3312/1/Hoyle.pdf.

[10] Quoted by Hugh Ross, *The Creator and the Cosmos*, 177.

"It seems as though someone has fine-tuned nature's numbers to make the Universe . . . The impression of design is overwhelming."[11]

Physicist Arno Penzias won the Nobel Prize for codiscovering echoes of the big bang in the form of background radiation. He states, "Astronomy leads us to a unique event, a Universe which was created out of nothing, one with the very delicate balance needed to provide exactly the right conditions required to permit life, and one which has an underlying (one might say 'supernatural') plan."[12] Likewise, cosmologist Bernard Carr states, "One would have to conclude either that the features of the universe invoked in support of the Anthropic Principle are only coincidences or that the universe was indeed tailor-made for life. I will leave it to the theologians to ascertain the identity of the tailor!"[13]

Not So Fast

Not everyone is convinced. Some contend that the fine-tuning arguments are the result of motivated reasoning and confirmation bias. An example of motivated reasoning would be someone who was such a fan of his favorite sports team that he ignores any faults the team might have. It's the danger of believing something so strongly that you only pay attention to the information that agrees with what you already think. You ignore anything that disagrees with your belief because you want to be

---

[11] Cited by John Lennox, *God's Undertaker*, 71.

[12] Lennox, 58.

[13] Ross, *The Creator and the Cosmos*, 178.

right or because it feels good to think that way. Imagine having a favorite puzzle piece that you like so much that you try to make every part of the picture fit that one piece.

Confirmation bias is a type of motivated reasoning. Imagine you're trying to prove that your favorite video game is the best one ever made. You might only look for reviews that give it high ratings and ignore the ones that point out any problems. You focus only on the information that agrees with what you already believe, and you ignore anything that might prove you wrong. Opponents of the fine-tuning argument contend that the theist sees evidence of fine-tuning because her biases have colored her perspective.

Motivated reasoning and confirmation bias are real human traits that need to be recognized. The possibility that such traits are playing a role has to be admitted. However, that doesn't seem to be what is happening in this case. First and foremost, the fine-tuning argument isn't about personal beliefs or subjective feelings; it's grounded in hard science. The constants that scientists discuss are well-established. These measurements are subjected to rigorous testing and verification by the scientific community.

Furthermore, the evidences for fine-tuning are not the products of biblical scholars and theologians. There's nothing in the biblical account of creation that requires fine-tuning. Scientists across the spectrum of religious beliefs have recognized the evidences, which demonstrates that the evidences are not merely products of a specific bias. In fact, many of the first proponents of fine-tuning resisted the results of their own research. Only after example after example was accumulated were they convinced that the phenomenon is real. It's a genuine scientific inquiry that transcends personal preferences or beliefs. Any complex topic, including this one, can be seen through different lenses, and people might apply their biases to it. That doesn't make the underlying scientific facts less valid.

Multiverse to the Rescue?

Most skeptics of fine-tuning do not contest the empirical evidence. Rather, they appeal to some version of multiverse theory, which they argue provides an alternative explanation for the apparent fine-tuning we observe. The multiverse theory posits that our universe is just one of an infinite number of universes, each with its own set of physical laws and constants. In such a vast or even infinite ensemble of universes, it's statistically likely that at least some universes would have the precise conditions necessary for life as we know it.

If we happen to find ourselves in a universe where the conditions are just right for our existence, it's not necessarily because those conditions were finely tuned for us. Rather, we observe these conditions simply because we exist in one of the universes where such conditions allow for our existence. In essence, our observation of fine-tuning could be a selection effect rather than evidence of deliberate design or special properties.

It's important to recognize that the multiverse hypothesis takes the conversation out of science and into the realm of metaphysics. In his book *Who's Afraid of the Multiverse?* astrophysicist Jeff Zweerink argues that even if the multiverse hypothesis is true, it works better in a Christian worldview than a materialist one. He points out that the multiverse requires a mechanism greater than multiverse itself.[14] Physicist Stephen M. Barr observes, "It is a very curious circumstance that materialists, in an effort to avoid what [French scholar Pierre-Simon] Laplace called the unnecessary hypothesis of God, are frequently driven to hypothesize the existence of an infinity of unobservable entities. . . . It seems that to abolish one unobservable God, it takes an infinite number of unobservable substitutes."[15] Let us remind ourselves of the definition of hypernaturalism. A hypernatural event is the point at which providence and miracles intersect. It is providential in the sense that it uses the laws of nature and natural mechanisms, but it is miraculous in the sense that its results go beyond what can be accounted for naturally.

In chapter 3 we considered the account of how Jesus provided the money to pay the temple tax for Simon Peter and himself (Matthew 17) by sending Peter to go fishing. Just as Jesus predicted, Peter found a gold coin in the mouth of the first fish he caught. It was not a miracle in the precise, supernatural sense of Jesus creating a coin that did not exist, but it could not be explained naturally either. The same holds true for fine-tuning.

The fine-tuning of the universe provides us with perhaps the clearest scientific example of hypernaturalism. Just like the story at the beginning of this chapter, if someone won every lottery every time, we would know that something else was going on besides normal, natural processes. Yet the evidence of fine-tuning demonstrates that we are the very fortunate winners of the cosmic lottery.

---

[14] Jeff Zweerink, *Who's Afraid of the Multiverse?* (Covina, CA: RTB, 2018), 7–9.

[15] Stephen M. Barr, *Modern Physics and Ancient Faith* (Notre Dame, IN: University of Notre Dame, 2003), 156–57.

6

The Rare Earth Hypothesis

There's No Place Like Home

I'm old enough to remember watching the original *Star Trek* series when it was first broadcast in 1966. As a little boy, I was thrilled by the way the show started with the starship *Enterprise* flying through space. Then came the dramatic voiceover by William Shatner, who played the star character, Captain Kirk: "Space: the final frontier. These are the voyages of the starship *Enterprise*. Its five-year mission: to explore strange new worlds, to seek out new life and new civilizations, to boldly go where no man has gone before!" The captain and his crew encountered Klingons, Vulcans, and numerous other intelligent beings. Every episode showcased new discoveries. Small wonder that the *Star Trek* franchise is still popular today.

The major assumption underlying *Star Trek* (and similar franchises such as *Star Wars* and *Dune*) is that the universe is teeming with other intelligent beings like us. A century ago, many science fiction stories involved aliens who lived on the other planets within our very own solar system. For example, in 1898 H. G. Wells wrote *War of the Worlds*, in which Martians invade our planet. At the time, the notion of complex life existing on Venus or Mars seemed like a very real possibility. But in the second half of the twentieth century, numerous satellites were sent to the other planets in the solar system. Now we know the disappointing reality that all of them are inhospitable to life (at least complex life).

We arrived at a similar verdict about much of the entire galaxy in which we live, the Milky Way. In fact, we now have determined that most galaxies—entire galaxies—exhibit properties that make it impossible for them to sustain complex life. Some scientists go so far as to contend that it's probable that the earth is the only place in the universe in which intelligent life exists. This theory is called the Rare Earth hypothesis.

The Demotion of Planet Earth

How important is Earth? To you and me it is obviously very important. But how important is it in the cosmic scheme of things? Generally, the ancient world viewed Earth as a rather insignificant place. Scripture presented a very different perspective: the biblical authors saw Earth as lovingly prepared for humanity by a gracious and good God. Now we understand that the universe is mind-blowingly huge. Once again, our planet seems to be just a drop of water in the cosmic ocean.

The Geocentric Universe

In the second century AD, the astronomer Claudius Ptolemy published *Almagest,* which presented a geocentric model of the universe. He placed the earth at the center, with the sun and planets revolving around the earth in larger and larger spheres. The outermost sphere was populated with the stars. His work was embraced almost universally by the scholars of his day, and the geocentric model became known as the Ptolemaic system.

What made Ptolemy's model so attractive was his introduction of the notion of "epicycles." From the earliest times the ancient astronomers noticed that, even though the planets generally traveled across the sky from west to east, occasionally they would reverse and briefly go backward. We now know that this is an optical illusion caused by the earth and the other planets orbiting the sun at different speeds and distances. Ptolemy's explanation was that each planet's trajectory included epicycles—small circular orbits—in addition to its larger orbit around the earth. The Ptolemaic system worked remarkably well, and it predicted planetary positions with a reasonable degree of accuracy.

Ptolemy, like most ancient scholars of his day, understood that the earth was a round sphere, but he did not see it as a planet (the word *planet* originally meant "a wanderer"). Our world was the bottom level of the created order. But this did not mean that the earth was insignificant. To the contrary, it may have occupied the lowest place in the cosmos, but it was also at the center. It was easy to view our world as having a purpose and place in the grand scheme of things. The medieval world viewed the earth as a stage in which a magnificent drama was being played out.

The Copernican Revolution

In 1543, Polish astronomer Nicolaus Copernicus (1473–1543) published *On the Revolutions of the Heavenly Spheres*, which argued for a heliocentric understanding of the solar system. The Copernican model placed the sun, rather than the earth, at the center and presented the earth, along with the other planets, as revolving around the sun. Subsequent astronomers like Galileo, Kepler, and Newton expanded upon and refined the heliocentric model, providing further evidence that the sun was indeed the center of the solar system.

The Copernican Revolution prompted a profound reevaluation of the significance of humans in the universe. Rather than being the center of the universe, the earth was just another planet—"a wanderer." It also meant that though the sun was central to our solar system, it was just one star among the billions and billions of stars in the Milky Way. Discoveries in the twentieth century of untold trillions of other galaxies and the immense, unfathomable size of the universe made the Milky Way seem small and maybe even trivial.

In light of the Copernican Revolution, astronomers embraced what came to be known as the Copernican Principle. The Copernican Principle states that there is no center to the universe; there is no privileged place. This means that the same laws of physics apply throughout the universe because we see it as it is seen anywhere else. The Copernican Principle also seems to imply that there's nothing special about our earth.

One of the earliest interplanetary satellites sent to explore the solar system was Voyager 1. In 1990, as the satellite was on its way out of our solar system, NASA's scientists directed it to angle its camera back at the earth. At an almost 4 billion-mile distance, our planet looked like a dim, blue speck set against the dark void of space. Because of the way the sunlight hit the camera's lens, the earth additionally appeared to be enveloped in a slender beam of light. In his book *Pale Blue Dot*, well-known astronomer and atheist Carl Sagan declared:

> Because of the reflection of sunlight off the spacecraft, the Earth seems to be sitting in a beam of light, as if there were some special significance to this small world. But it is just an accident of geometry and optics. . . . Our posturings, our imagined self-importance, the delusion that we have some privileged position in the Universe, are challenged by this point of pale light. Our planet is a lonely speck in the great enveloping cosmic dark. In our obscurity, in all this vastness, there is no hint that help will come from elsewhere to save us from ourselves.[1]

Sagan summed up the modern conviction that the earth is all alone and insignificant. However, at this time another very different hypothesis was making its way through astronomical circles. Many scientists were beginning to realize that the earth is very special indeed.

The Recognition of the Rare Earth

How things have changed in the past fifty years! The realization was gradual at first, but lately the awareness has become broad and pervasive. Today there is nearly universal agreement that we live on a spectacularly amazing planet.

---

[1] Carl Sagan, *Pale Blue Dot: A Vision of the Human Future in Space* (New York: Random House, 1994), 5–7. My attention was drawn to this quote by William Dembski's book, *The End of Christianity* (Nashville: B&H Academic, 2009), 41.

The Drake Equation and the Fermi Paradox

In 1961, astronomer Frank Drake proposed a probabilistic equation for estimating the number of technologically advanced civilizations that might exist in the Milky Way galaxy. The equation itself is expressed as $N = R^* \bullet f_p \bullet n_e \bullet f_l \bullet f_i \bullet f_c \bullet L$, where

- N is the number of civilizations we might be able to communicate with,
- R^* is the average rate of star formation per year,
- f_p is the fraction of those stars that have planets,
- n_e is the average number of planets that can support life per star with planets,
- f_l is the fraction of those planets that develop life,
- f_i is the fraction of those planets with intelligent life,
- f_c is the fraction of those civilizations that develop technology to communicate across interstellar distances,
- L is the length of time those civilizations are communicating.

Using the best estimates of the time, Drake concluded that it was likely that over 10,000 advanced civilizations inhabit the Milky Way galaxy. His calculations were a major impetus for the SETI project (Search for Extraterrestrial Intelligence). Using radio telescopes and other similar devices, SETI has scanned millions of stars in search of indications of intelligent life.

Though the Drake equation indicates that there should be many planets hosting advanced, complex beings, it seems to have run head-on into the Fermi paradox. Physicist Enrico Fermi (1901–54) was in an informal conversation with other scientists about UFOs and extraterrestrials when he was supposed to have blurted out, "But where is everybody?" His now-famous question has come to be known as the Fermi paradox, the seeming contradiction between the high probability of the existence of intelligent life and the lack of evidence or contact with such civilizations.

Our Special Little Corner of the Universe

There is increasing awareness that we live in a universe that, for the most part, is highly inhospitable to life. The brutal conditions of outer space, stars, and planets appear overwhelmingly harsh. One popular scientist describes things thus: "The universe is a deadly place. At every opportunity it's trying to kill us."[2] The more we know about the cosmos, the more we realize just how special our little planet really is. And not just our planet—it appears that we live in a special solar system after all. Even the Milky Way turns out to be unique.

In the previous chapter we discussed the fine-tuning argument and looked at the many evidences that the constants of the universe seem to be calibrated very closely so that life might exist somewhere. We saw that there is a plethora of books published by scientists, each providing a barrage of examples. In a similar way, numerous astronomers and other scientists are writing about the Rare Earth hypothesis. Geologist Peter Ward and astronomer Donald Brownlee have written *Rare Earth: Why Complex Life Is So Uncommon in the Universe,* while

---

[2] "(Caught on Camera): The Universe is Trying to Kill You | Big Think," YouTube video, 0:35, n.d., https://www.youtube.com/watch?v=Fw62e4SDHHo.

astronomer Guillermo Gonzalez and philosopher Jay Wesley Richards have authored *The Privileged Planet: How Our Place in the Cosmos Is Designed for Discovery*. In addition, astronomer Hugh Ross has written several books on the topic, including *Designed to the Core*. And they provide a similar phalanx of examples. Here are a few of the more salient ones.[3]

First, the positioning of the earth's orbit within the solar system appears to be precisely correct. Given the sun's characteristics—including its size and energy output—there exists only a somewhat limited zone where the earth could be situated and remain suitable for life. The exact distance between the earth and the sun has proven to be ideal. Initial research suggested that if the earth were merely 1 percent closer to the sun, the extra heat would result in the complete evaporation of the ocean. Conversely, if the earth were 5 percent farther from the sun, the oceans would become entirely frozen. As described by Hugh Ross, the earth's biosphere is "poised between a runaway freeze-up and a runaway evaporation."[4] Moreover, the mean temperature needs to be at a point where water would stay, while other greenhouse gases like methane and ammonia would mainly vanish. Although more recent research indicates that the acceptable range might be more extensive than first thought, the habitable zone continues to be "quite narrow."[5]

---

[3] The following examples are adapted from my book *40 Questions about Creation and Evolution* (Grand Rapids, MI: Kregel, 2010), 403–7.

[4] Hugh Ross, *The Creator and the Cosmos: How the Latest Discoveries Reveal God* (Covina, CA: RTB, 2018), 127.

[5] Peter D. Ward and Donald Brownlee, *Rare Earth: Why Complex Life Is Uncommon in the Universe* (Göttingen: Copernicus, 2003), 18.

Second, our planet displays specific traits that make it distinctively suited for life. For instance, the earth is currently the sole planet in our solar system with the phenomenon of plate tectonics.[6] While they can cause earthquakes, plate tectonics are unexpectedly vital in supporting life. They are instrumental in keeping global temperatures steady and ensuring a stable oceanic environment. Another distinctive feature of the earth is its sizable lunar companion. Uniquely large for a planet of the earth's dimensions, the moon is a quarter the size of the earth, whereas other planets' moons are much smaller relative to the size of their planets. In combination with elements like plate tectonics, the moon's effect on the earth's orientation and rotation contributes to stabilizing our planet's temperature. It helps maintain the earth's axial tilt near twenty-three degrees; and without the moon, the earth's rotation would be unsteady and wobbly.

The instances mentioned in the preceding paragraph represent just a small selection of many that could be pointed out, yet they convey the general concept. In *The Creator and the Cosmos*, Hugh Ross identifies thirty-three specific conditions that a planet must satisfy to harbor life. According to his calculations, the chance of one planet fulfilling all thirty-three of these requirements is 1 in 10^{-42}. Contrastingly, the upper limit of possible planets, as estimated by astronomers, is 10^{22}. Ross summarizes the likelihood of a planet like earth existing by random occurrence as being "much less than one in a quintillion."[7] Thus, it becomes evident that our terrestrial ball is indeed a remarkably unique location.

---

[6] Ward and Brownlee, 220.

[7] Ross, *Creator and the Cosmos*, 134.

Third, our sun itself is just right for habitable life on earth. Contrary to what many astronomy textbooks might suggest, painting the sun as an ordinary and unremarkable star, Ward and Brownlee argue that our sun is far from typical. Instead of being an average star, it's larger than 95 percent of all stars. In reality, most stars fall into the M-class category (stars that are a mere 10 percent of the size of the sun), further emphasizing the sun's uniqueness.[8]

If the sun were smaller than its current size, its habitable zone would consequently shrink, necessitating the earth to orbit more closely. This closer orbit would lead to the sun's gravity having a significantly increased influence on the earth's rotation period. In essence, instead of completing a rotation every twenty-four hours, the earth's rotation would decelerate to the point where it would complete only one rotation annually. This would make the earth's rotation akin to Mercury's, the planet closest to the sun, which rotates just one and a half times during each orbit around the sun. This effect is the same as how the earth's gravity impacts the moon, causing it to rotate only once during each orbit around the earth (i.e., once a month), allowing us to see only one side of the moon (the other side being visible only during the lunar cycle's dark phase). The final consequence of earth's closer orbit to the sun would be that one side would consistently face intense solar heat for prolonged durations, becoming hundreds of degrees hot, while the dark side would plummet to hundreds of degrees below zero (conditions found on Mercury). Such extreme conditions would render life on the earth impossible.[9]

---

[8] Ward and Brownlee, *Rare Earth*, 23. "It is often said that the sun is a typical star, but this is entirely untrue."

[9] Ward and Brownlee, 23–24.

However, if the sun were much larger than it is, the consequences for life would be just as disastrous. A sun of greater size would emit substantially higher amounts of ultraviolet light, levels that would indeed be too intense for life to endure. Life on the earth thrives because of a "Goldilocks star," one that is neither too small nor too large but just right.[10] The sun's contribution to the earth goes beyond the sun's dimensions. In the Milky Way, the majority of stars similar to the sun (80 to 85 percent) are either binary stars or part of clusters containing three or more stars. Planets that orbit binary stars experience orbits that are too unstable to create the consistent and moderate conditions required for life, and the energy these planets receive fluctuates excessively. The uniqueness of our sun, being solitary rather than part of a binary or multiple star system, is a crucial characteristic that makes life possible.[11]

Fourth, our neighboring planets happen to be precisely what the earth needs. The existence of large planets like Jupiter and Saturn, patrolling the outer solar system, helps to keep the earth relatively safe. Both of these planets are essential, as their correct size and distance from each other ensure that they maintain a stable orbit. If either Jupiter or Saturn were significantly different, Jupiter could potentially eject Saturn from the solar system and could itself enter an elliptical orbit, leading to an eventual collision with the earth.[12] As it stands, Jupiter functions as a sort of cosmic vacuum cleaner for the earth, capturing space debris. Without Jupiter, the earth in the early days of the solar system would have been hit by space debris at a

[10] Ward and Brownlee, 22.

[11] Ward and Brownlee, 25.

[12] Ward and Brownlee, 21–22.

rate that's 10,000 times higher than the current rate. Currently, "extinction-causing projectiles" impact the earth roughly once every 100 million years. Without Jupiter's protective presence, this rate would increase to once every 10,000 years, a frequency too high for life to adequately recover.[13]

Fifth, the earth's position in the Milky Way galaxy is perfectly suited for life. Eighty-five thousand light-years in width, the Milky Way finds the earth situated approximately twenty-five thousand light-years from its center, a location that is incredibly favorable for sustaining life. Similar to the habitable zone in our solar system, our galaxy also has a region that supports life.[14] If we were situated closer to the Milky Way's center, we would be exposed to harmful cosmic rays and particles from exploding supernovae. Conversely, being farther from the center would mean a lack of heavy elements essential for life, as the outer bands of the galaxy are composed mainly of hydrogen and helium, with vital elements like oxygen, nitrogen, carbon, iron, and others missing. Earth's position strikes the perfect balance, being distant enough from the center to avoid most of the harmful radiation yet close enough to ensure the availability of all the crucial elements needed for life.

Our Galaxy

Galaxies are primarily classified according to three types: spiral, elliptical, and irregular.[15] The Milky Way is a vast spiral galaxy

---

[13] Ward and Brownlee, 238–39.

[14] Ward and Brownlee, 27.

[15] Guillermo Gonzalez and Jay W. Richards, *Privileged Planet: How Our Place in the Cosmos Is Designed for Discovery* (Washington, DC: Regnery, 2020), 144.

featuring significant arms filled with stars and dust. Our specific location within the Milky Way is in a relatively uncluttered area (with our closest star being four light-years away), nestled between two of these spiral arms. Unlike our relatively isolated location, most stars are found in dense globular clusters, containing tens of thousands of stars within a confined space, mainly within the spiral arms. Planets within these clusters would be subjected to relentless radiation and particle bombardments, rendering life untenable.[16] Fortunately, the earth's position in an open space between the spiral arms protects us from this intense onslaught, allowing for the possibility of life.

And sixth, our Milky Way galaxy is just right. At the center of every galaxy is a supermassive black hole. As Hugh Ross explains, for the vast majority of galaxies, these black holes are active.[17] By active, he means that on regular occasions (about every 100,000 years) they suck in stars that orbit too close to the black hole. As a star is consumed by a black hole, it emits an unimaginable amount of energy in the form of gamma radiation. This radiation is so intense that it would kill not only all life that might exist in that galaxy but also any life unfortunate enough to live in a nearby galaxy. For example, one of our relatively nearby galaxies is M-87, located about 50 million light-years from us. Its extremely active supermassive black hole guarantees that, as far

---

[16] Ward and Brownlee, *Rare Earth*, 25–27. Evidently our solar system originated in a violent, metal-rich part of the Milky Way but was then slung out to the relatively safe place it resides today. See Jeff Zweerink, "Solar System Turns Out Well Despite Violent Birthplace," https://reasons.org/explore/publications/articles/solar-system-turns-out-well-despite-violent-birthplace.

[17] Hugh Ross, *Designed to the Core* (Covina, CA: RTB, 2022), 97–101.

a biological life is concerned, the entire galaxy is sterile and barren. We are fortunate that M-87 is not any closer, or else there would be no life on earth or anywhere else in the Milky Way.

Fortunately for us, the supermassive black hole at the center of our Milky Way galaxy is dormant. As Ross explains, the black hole engages only in "minimal consumption, comparable to light snacking."[18] Earth is like a peaceful village, snuggled at the base of a massive but extinct volcano. There really is no place like home.

We began this chapter by recounting the words that William Shatner spoke at the opening of *Star Trek*. In 2021, he flew above Earth's atmosphere aboard the spaceship *Blue Origin*. At ninety, Shatner was the oldest astronaut at the time to journey into outer space. The trip did not have the effect on him that he expected.

Shatner thought that he would feel the exhilaration of "going boldly where no one had gone before." Instead he was struck by the stark contrast between the warm beauty of our planet and the menacing, inky darkness of space. Then he felt what he described as "the deepest grief I had ever experienced." In a news article he explained:

> While I was looking away from Earth, and turned towards the rest of the universe, I didn't feel connection; I didn't feel attraction. What I understood, in the clearest possible way, was that we were living on a tiny oasis of life, surrounded by an immensity of death. I didn't see infinite possibilities of worlds to explore, of adventures to have, or living creatures to connect with.

---

[18] Ross, 99.

> I saw the deepest darkness I could have ever imagined, contrasting starkly with the welcoming warmth of our nurturing home planet.[19]

Shatner concluded with an appeal to care for our privileged planet. We may not live in the literal center of the universe, as the Ptolemaic model taught, but it is obvious we inhabit a place that enjoys a very special providential care.

---

[19] William Shatner, "My Trip to Space Made Me Realise We Have Only One Earth—It Must Live Long and Prosper," *Guardian* (UK), December 7, 2022, https://www.theguardian.com/environment/2022/dec/07/william-shatner-earth-must-live-long-and-prosper-aoe.

7

The Origin of Life

How did life on earth begin? In Genesis 1, Moses paints a vivid picture of God's purposeful, comprehensive creation of all life. Genesis 1:11–26 details the creation of life in a series of stages, each with its own particular focus. Young-earth creationists (YEC) understand the days of creation to be actual twenty-four-hour days that occurred fewer than 10,000 years ago, while old-earth creationists (OEC) generally interpret Genesis 1 either to be presenting the six stages of creation (i.e., the "day-age hypothesis") or to be depicting a thematic framework (the "framework hypothesis"). Evolutionary creationists (EC) typically understand the creation account to be a metaphorical telling, accommodated to the limitations of the ancient understanding of the world.

All creationists agree that Genesis showcases a purposeful and systematic creation where every form of life—whether on land, in the sea, or in the air—is crafted with intention and care. It presents God as the master Designer, capable of orchestrating the complexities of the entire ecosystem. This world was created by a wise, good, and sovereign God, and it manifests his genius and his glory.

Those who wish to explore the origin of life from a purely naturalistic perspective find themselves in a conundrum. How could life come from nonlife? When and where did life happen? One of the great scientific mysteries is how life started on planet Earth, and it involves a field of study called "abiogenesis." Current theories hypothesize that around 3.5 to 4 billion years ago, the earth's primitive environment contained simple organic compounds like amino acids and nucleotides. Through a series of complex chemical reactions (possibly triggered by environmental factors such as lightning, volcanic activity, or deep-sea hydrothermal vents), these molecules combined and recombined to form more complex structures like proteins and ribonucleic acid (RNA). Over time, these macromolecules might have organized into self-replicating systems, eventually leading to the first primitive cells. At least, that's the theory. The complexity of even the simplest cell is staggering. No attempts so far have succeeded in recreating a step-by-step process that would explain how life might have originated.

The Wonderful World of Spontaneous Generation

The idea that nonlife can, under certain circumstances, produce life is called "spontaneous generation." In his book, *Creatures Born of Mud and Slime,* philosopher Daryn Lehoux declares that all proponents of abiogenesis believe that spontaneous generation must have happened at least once: "Somewhere in this marvelous universe of ours, at least once in its 13.8-billion-year history, life came into being from nonliving matter through some kind of chemical process. We don't yet know where or when this happened, but the fact that we are here to think about it at all is a trivial—but quite definitive—proof that it did."[1] Lehoux's logic seems clear enough. If materialism is one's starting point, our mere existence requires the materialist to embrace some version of spontaneous generation. From the time of the ancient Greek philosophers until the nineteenth century, many believed that nonliving elements regularly produced living creatures. In ancient times, it was believed that larger creatures, including even humans, could spontaneously emerge from nonliving matter. As time progressed, this idea was refined, and the focus shifted to smaller organisms and then to even tinier forms of life. Eventually, the concept was narrowed to the belief that at least microscopic entities, such as microbes, could arise spontaneously.

Ancient Beliefs about Spontaneous Generation

The Roman poet Lucretius (c.99–c.55 BC) argued for a crude form of spontaneous generation. In his poem *The Nature of Things*, he argued that the universe is made up of only two things: an infinite number of minute atoms and an infinite void. These atoms have a variety of shapes, and, given an infinite amount of time, they will eventually come together to create life. (Think of the analogy of an infinite number of monkeys typing on keyboards for an infinite amount of time. Eventually one of them will replicate all the works of Shakespeare. Same idea here.) Lucretius explains, "For there are many creatures

---

[1] Daryn Lehoux, *Creatures Born of Mud and Slime: The Wonder and Complexity of Spontaneous Generation* (Baltimore: Johns Hopkins University, 2017), 10.

even now that spring to birth/ From soil that's sodden by the rain, coddled by sunny warmth,/ So it's no wonder more and larger creatures at that time/ Sprang from the soil when Earth and Air were still fresh in their prime."[2] He reasoned that, given an eternity's worth of time, eventually everything that could be created would be, including humans.

Though several ancient philosophers affirmed spontaneous generation, none explored the notion as thoroughly as Aristotle (394–322 BC). In his book *The Generation of Animals,* he carefully recounted what he believed to be clear evidence that mud and slime produced frogs, fish, and eels. Aristotle argued that primal elements came together to produce the different species and that the elements contained vital forces that can create life.[3]

Belief in Spontaneous Generation throughout the Scientific Revolution

Aristotle's views held sway throughout the medieval period. Scholars during this time offered precise formulas for producing certain creatures: rotting hay birthed mice, decomposing cows generated bees, and dead horses produced wasps. Crocodiles arose from mud, while geese developed from barnacles.

By the seventeenth century, several scholars were expressing doubts about the viability of spontaneous generation. The Italian physician Francesco Redi (1626–97) challenged the

---

[2] Lucretius, *The Nature of Things,* trans. A. E. Stallings (New York: Penguin, 2007), 5.790–810.

[3] Lehoux, *Creatures Born of Mud and Slime*, 51–64.

notion that rotting meat spontaneously produced maggots. He conducted a series of experiments using jars of meat, some that were sealed and others that were uncovered. Redi demonstrated that maggots appeared only in the open jars—jars in which flies could lay their eggs.

Nevertheless, belief in spontaneous generation persisted throughout the eighteenth and nineteenth centuries. The English biologist John Turberville Needham (1713–81) conducted a series of experiments that he believed refuted Redi's results. He boiled broth and then sealed it in containers. When he observed the growth of microorganisms, he claimed that "vital forces" in the broth gave rise to life. Others disagreed, correctly suggesting that the broth must have been contaminated before sealing.

One of the most influential advocates of spontaneous generation was the French naturalist Georges-Louis Leclerc, Comte de Buffon (1707–88), known for his thirty-six-volume encyclopedia of science, *Histoire Naturelle*. He argued that under the right conditions life springs up fully formed and that it happens regularly and often. Buffon's views held sway over many of the Enlightenment thinkers of his day.

Then in the 1850s, the brilliant French chemist Louis Pasteur (1822–95) decisively refuted spontaneous generation through a series of meticulous experiments. By using swan-necked flasks, he was able to allow air but not microorganisms into sterilized broths. These controlled conditions demonstrated that without contamination, no microbial life developed in the broth. Pasteur's results not only disproved spontaneous generation but also laid the groundwork for the modern germ theory of disease.

It's worth noting that all the various theories of spontaneous generation had one thing in common. Whether ancient or modern, crude or sophisticated, all theories assumed that creating life from nonlife was a relatively easy endeavor. Today we realize that this notion is not only wrong; it is spectacularly wrong.

The Discovery of Cells and DNA

By the start of the twentieth century, spontaneous generation was universally considered to be a discredited idea. However, there was one way it was still believed that life arose from nonlife: the origin of the cell.

The Discovery of the "Little Rooms"

In 1590 the microscope was invented in Holland. In 1665, the English scientist Robert Hooke used the new device to look at a thin slice of cork. He saw small, box-like structures that reminded him of the small rooms, or "cells" in monasteries, so that's what he called them. This was the discovery of cells. Cells quickly came to be understood as the fundamental units of life. All living organisms are either single-cell microbes or multicellular complex creatures. Cells are the basic building blocks of everything alive.

From the time of their discovery until the twentieth century, cells were believed to be relatively simple things. In the nineteenth century, scientists theorized that cells contained "protoplasm." Protoplasm was understood to be a viscous, jelly-like substance made up primarily of water, nitrogen, and simple hydrocarbons. Jay Richards explains, "Biologists believed that the cell was a simple homogenous globule of protoplasm—like a simple glob of green gelatin."[4] According to the early theories, cells were merely tiny packets of protoplasm. Early Darwinists, such as Thomas Huxley and Ernst Haeckel, argued that these protoplasmic cells evolved easily. Haeckel explains: "Organisms which are, in fact, not composed of any organs at all, but consist entirely of shapeless, simple, homogeneous matter. The entire body of one of these Monera, during life, is nothing more than a shapeless, mobile, little lump of mucus or slime, consisting of an albuminous combination of carbon. Simpler or more imperfect organisms we cannot possibly conceive."[5] However, by the beginning of the twentieth century, scientists were realizing that cells are anything but simple, and so the protoplasmic theory of the cell fell into disfavor.

The Discovery of the DNA Molecule

In 1943, the renowned physicist Erwin Schrödinger gave a series of lectures that were published as a book titled *What Is Life?* He proposed that cells might contain an "aperiodic crystal" that could carry genetic information as some type of code or formula.[6] He speculated that this unique molecule would have to be complex and capable of conveying specific information. Inspired by

---

[4] Jay Richards, "Why Are We Here? Accident or Purpose?" in *Intelligent Design 101: Leading Experts Explain the Key Issues*, ed. H. Wayne House (Grand Rapids, MI: Kregel, 2008), 135.

[5] Ernst Haeckel, *The History of Creation: or The Development of the Earth and Its Inhabitants by the Actions of Natural Causes* (New York: Appleton, 1880), 184. Available online: http://www.gutenberg.org/files/40472/40472-h/40472-h.htm.

[6] Erwin Schrödinger, *What Is Life?: With Mind and Matter and Autobiographical Sketches* (Cambridge, UK: Cambridge University Press, 2012), 5.

Schrödinger and using the work of Rosalind Franklin, a decade later James Watson and Francis Crick discovered the famous double-helix nature of the DNA (deoxyribonucleic acid) molecule. Research in genetics and microbiology then exploded.

The Hypernatural World of the Cell

But where did the very first cell come from? This brings us back to our original question: How did life on Earth begin?

There's Nothing Simple about Life

Cells and DNA are ubiquitous. All life is either single-cell organisms or creatures composed of a complex amalgamation of cells. At the moment of your conception, you were a single cell, which then immediately started to multiply by dividing. By the time your mother gave birth to you, you had become the multi-trillion-celled person you are now. At the center of each of your cells resides the DNA molecule.

Each cell is incredibly, unimaginably complex. Scientists describe the cell as more complicated than the most bustling metropolis and more intricate than the most advanced computer chip. In his book, *The Fifth Miracle: The Search for the Origin and Meaning of Life,* physicist Paul Davies describes cells in hushed, almost reverent terms:

> Peering into life's innermost workings serves only to deepen the mystery. The living cell is the most complex system of its size known to mankind. Its host of specialized molecules, many found nowhere else but within living material, are themselves already enormously complex. They execute a dance of exquisite fidelity,

orchestrated with breathtaking precision. Vastly more elaborate than the most complicated ballet, the dance of life encompasses countless molecular performers in synergetic coordination.[7]

What Is the Source of DNA's Information?

At the center of every cell resides the DNA molecule—a double helix composed of several billion atoms. Even though cells are so small that they can't be seen with the human eye, the DNA molecule is remarkably long—more than six feet in length. It manages to fit within the cell by twisting into an amazingly convoluted shape.

The DNA molecule is rich in information. The origin of this information has been a mystery that scientists have struggled to solve ever since its discovery. As Stephen Meyer explains, often this type of information is called "specified complexity." Specified complexity is both ordered and varied. This page that you are reading is an example of specified complexity. What if this page was simply a mad jumble of symbols, numbers, and letters? Consider the following line of text:

;alsdkfjqp4958_)(*z/cvmeleev naewf;vmvmvs;ladkfj

The above line is certainly complex, but it's also incomprehensible. But what if the "A" key on my keyboard got stuck, so that the only thing on this page was the letter A—just row after row of "A."

AAAAAAAAAAAAAAAAAAAAAAAAAAAAAA

I could continue to type "A," but you get the idea. The page would be orderly, even specific. But just like the jumbled-up text,

---

[7] Paul Davies, *The Fifth Miracle: The Search for the Origin and Meaning of Life* (New York: Simon and Schuster, 1999), 29.

it would communicate little in the way of information. The reason you can read and comprehend what I've written is because we are both following the rules for understanding English writing. Information only can be communicated via specified complexity: a narrow, orderly set of rules that allow for creativity and novelty. Biological life requires the same type of specified complexity that is found in DNA and other parts of the cell.

What are the odds of just one functional protein of the DNA molecule coming about by chance alone? Meyer does the math:

> My calculations are based upon recent experiments in molecular biology establishing the extreme rarity of functional proteins in relation to the total number of possible arrangements of amino acids corresponding to a protein of a given length. Taking that and several other relevant independent factors into account, I show that the probability of producing even a single functional protein of modest length (150 amino acids) by chance alone in a prebiotic environment stands at no better than a "vanishingly small" 1 chance in 10^{164}, an inconceivably small probability. To put this number in perspective, recall that physicists estimate that there are only 10^{80} elementary particles in the entire universe.[8]

This is why Meyer calls the origin of information "the DNA enigma."

---

[8] Stephen C. Meyer, *Return of the God Hypothesis: Three Scientific Discoveries That Reveal the Mind Behind the Universe* (New York: HarperOne, 2023), 271. Meyer's calculations give the possible number of proteins. Those actually existing in nature are estimated to be between 10^3 and 10^6. See Fazale Rana, "Just-Right RNA Structure Points to Intentional Design," https://reasons.org/explore/blogs/the-cells-design/just-right-rna-structure-points-to-intentional-design.

The Chicken or the Egg?

Another question that comes up when considering the origin of life is which came first: cells or the DNA molecule? DNA can instruct cells to replicate, but it can't create cells. And cells cannot function without DNA. So, cells and DNA have a symbiotic relationship—one requires the other. This means that the first, original cell—no matter how primitive it might have been—was unimaginably complex.

Several molecules contained inside cells are found nowhere else but within cells. In other words, it appears that the only thing that can produce those molecules is something that is already living. And these molecules are not superfluous; they are essential for cells to function.[9] So how would they have come about in the first place?

Is This a Case of Biological Fine-Tuning?

In chapter 5 we examined how the cosmological constants appear to be finely tuned for life to exist. Paleobiologist Simon Conway-Morris argues that the biological parameters seem to be just as finely tuned as the cosmological ones, maybe even more so. Life on earth, Conway-Morris explains, tiptoes on "the knife edge of biological existence."[10] At the molecular level, chemistry presents biological life with two side-by-side

---

[9] Fazale Rana and Hugh Ross, *Origins of Life: Biblical and Evolutionary Models Face Off* (Colorado Springs: NavPress, 2014), 132–33.

[10] Simon Conway-Morris, *From Extraterrestrials to Animal Minds* (West Conshohocken, PA: Templeton, 2022), 87.

sets of possibilities: chaos and rigidity. Both sets are so immense as to be practically infinite. Each set is a "desolate landscape of nonviability." Together, they present "two grim faces" that are "immense wastes of nonviability, where nothing biological will ever work." On one side of the knife edge is total chaos, disorder, and anarchy. The gaslike, constantly turbulent, tumbling molecular action guarantees that even if an orderly combination did come together by chance, it would be quickly torn apart by the same unending forces that brought them together.

On the other side of the knife edge is the exact opposite. Instead of chaos there is rigidity. Everything is the same, unchanging and frozen: "There is too much order, a crystalline-like world where everything is locked into immobility," writes Conway-Morris. No development, improvement, or progress is possible. He goes on to explain, "This in turn hints at the real nature of the unimaginable vastness of biological hyperspace, with its potentially almost infinite number of alternative possibilities. They may be mathematically imaginable, but practically all are biologically uninhabitable."[11]

Now imagine the border where the two realms meet. This boundary is razor thin, a fine line that acts as a partition between the two realms. This sliver is where biological life on earth resides; in fact, it is the only place where life is even possible. In this border area both order and development can coexist. Within this narrow range the high levels of information necessary for life can survive, replicate, and develop. Conway-Morris observes, "The infinitesimal fraction of vitality in the

[11] Conway-Morris, 66.

hyperspace is so specific that it might in turn point to a deeper order of the world."[12]

A Question of Timing

In their book *Origins of Life,* biochemist Fuz Rana and astronomer Hugh Ross argue that, geologically speaking, life appears to have arrived on the earth almost as soon as Earth came into existence.[13] According to standard geological models, our planet is approximately 4.5 billion years old. For the first 600 million years, Earth was a brutal, inhospitable place of molten lava and was frequently bombarded by asteroids. In fact, this period was so hellish that geologists called it the "Hadean era" (referring to Hades). Up until 3.9 billion years ago, life on earth was impossible. Yet the fossil record indicates that life began to exist no later than 3.8 billion years ago—leaving a window of only 100 million years for life to arise. As Rana and Ross observe, "Life appeared on Earth in a geological moment. The instant permanent rocks formed, life burst forth."[14]

Scientists have been working for over 100 years to formulate a plausible account of the first living cell, and they appear to be no closer today than they have ever been. Davies concludes that no currently known scientific processes can account for life. He declares:

> The peculiarity of biological complexity makes genes seem almost like impossible objects—yet they must

---

[12] Conway-Morris, 66.

[13] Rana and Ross, *Origins of Life*, 85.

[14] Rana and Ross, 85.

> have formed somehow. I have come to the conclusion that no familiar law of nature could produce such a structure from incoherent chemicals with the inevitability that some scientists assert. If life does form easily, and is common throughout the universe, then new physical principles must be at work.[15]

Conway-Morris observes, "It is certainly not my intention to suggest that the origin of life is a scientifically intractable problem, but at this stage of the proceedings simply to register mild surprise at the relative lack of experimental success."[16] After giving a history of "origin of life" experiments, Conway-Morris, quoting biochemistry educator Klaus Dose, describes the results as a "catalogue of disasters." Dose concludes, "It appears that the field has now reached a stage of stalemate."[17]

God of the Gaps?

Often at this point in origin of life discussions, an objector warns about the danger of making a "God of the gaps" argument. A "God of the gaps" argument is a theological appeal to ignorance, where gaps in scientific understanding are attributed to miracles. Essentially, if there's something that science can't yet explain, this approach fills that gap with the explanation that "God did it." The obvious risk of this approach is that it relies on the current limitations of scientific understanding. Typically, "God of the gaps" arguments eventually backfire because, as

---

[15] Davies, *The Fifth Miracle*, 20.

[16] Simon Conway-Morris, *Life's Solution: Inevitable Humans in a Lonely Universe* (New York: Cambridge University, 2003), 44–49.

[17] Dose, in Conway-Morris, 48.

science progresses and fills in those gaps with natural explanations, the space for the divine explanation shrinks.

So, is the discussion on the mystery of life's origin an appeal to ignorance? Well, yes and no. Yes, obviously we are pointing to something that science has yet to explain; but no, this is not *merely* an appeal to ignorance. In many ways it is the exact opposite. It appears that the more science learns about the cell, the more intractable the problem of its origin becomes. The more our understanding has improved, the more it has deepened the mystery. Origin of life research resembles Aristotle's beliefs more and more: the belief that creatures of immense complexity spontaneously generated.

It is important to remember that hypernaturalism does not merely appeal to the miraculous in the direct, first-order sense. A major thesis of this book is that God often works in the realm between naturalism and supernaturalism. Perhaps future paleobiologists will be able to formulate a theory that accounts for how life began. However, if such a theory could be formulated (and that's a big *if*), all indications are that the solution would point to an extraordinarily fortuitous event, so improbable that it staggers the imagination. Such a theory would be the very definition of a hypernatural event.

8

The Hypernatural World of Biology

Physics has black holes, relativity, and the surreal world of quantum mechanics, but when it comes to sheer complexity, biology wins hands down. As we saw in chapter 5 on fine-tuning, astrophysics deals with numbers that are incomprehensibly large. Yet biology deals with numbers that are unimaginably larger. For example, the number of the possible combinations of amino acids (the building blocks of proteins) is greater than the number of atoms in the universe.[1]

Biology Is Messy

Aside from enormous numbers, biology is messy for other reasons. One of the integral features of living systems is the shuffling and sorting process that utilizes randomness and chance.

---

[1] Stephen Meyer, *Return of the God Hypothesis: Three Scientific Discoveries That Reveal the Mind Behind the Universe* (New York: HarperOne, 2023), 311–12.

The study of stochastic processes (i.e., randomness, probability, and chance) is a well-developed area of mathematics that has many applications in the field of biology. The inherently contingent nature of the biological realm makes it unpredictable. Astronomers can predict millions of years in advance the location of the sun in the Milky Way; biologists can make no such predictions about living things. Life on earth is simply too complex. For some Christians, randomness seems to be at odds with the Christian view of providence, but we will see that this is not the case at all.

Ethical concerns emerge from the very processes of biology and make the field of biology messy in ways not apparent in the other natural sciences. Predation, selfishness, and suffering are the norm for living things. We feel no qualms when a black hole gobbles up a neutron star. But when a killer whale eats a baby seal—even though we realize that's just the way of nature—we empathize with the little seal.

Ever since Charles Darwin published *On the Origin of Species* (1859), in which he (along with Alfred Russel Wallace) proposed evolution by means of natural selection, the perception has been that there is an irreconcilable tension between the Christian faith and the field of biology. This is not entirely unjustified. However, a number of interesting developments indicate that the breach is not as large as some would have us believe, nor are the problems insurmountable.

Christianity presents two foundational truths about biological life. First, all life has its origin in God. He called upon the ground to bring forth vegetation, the seas and skies to swarm with creatures that swim and fly respectively, and the earth to produce creatures that move across its surface (Gen 1:11–24).

Second, though humans are connected to the earth and other creatures, they are also unique. Humans are the special creation of God. We were made in God's image; thus, we are reflectors of the divine imprint. How does the biblical vision of purposeful creation square with the messiness found in biology?

Providence and Random Chance

Is our existence the result of intelligent design or random chance? The question pits design and chance against each other. We see this in the loaded terms like *purpose* and *design* countered by *randomness* and *chance*. One can find many instances of leading thinkers taking this adversarial approach. For example, the mathematician Bertrand Russell stated, "Man is the product of causes which had no prevision of the end they were achieving."[2] Or as paleontologist George Gaylord Simpson expressed it, "Man is the result of a purposeless and natural process that did not have him in mind."[3] In other words, Russell and Simpson conclude that we are the result of chance, not purpose.

With all due respect to Russell and Simpson, there is a very good reason the processes that brought us about did not have us in mind. Of course they didn't have us in mind! Processes don't have minds. The electrical processes that light our homes do

---

[2] See Bertrand Russell, "A Free Man's Worship," in Russell, *Mysticism and Logic and Other Essays* (London: Richard Clay, 1918), 46–57.

[3] Simpson, quoted in Ann Gauger, Douglas Axe, and Casey Luskin, *Science and Human Origins* (Seattle: Discovery Institute, 2012), 9.

not have us in mind, neither do the mechanical processes that enable us to travel in cars. Nor did the biochemical processes that caused you to gestate in your mother's womb. The real question is whether or not there is a Mind behind the process.

Minds can have good reasons for employing random processes. Consider card games. Virtually every card game begins with the deck being shuffled. The six of diamonds doesn't have the players in mind, nor does the act of shuffling. But the rules of the game and the game's intended outcome are designed very much with the players in mind. The process of randomization—the shuffling of the deck—is part of the game plan and is essential to the game's desired outcome. Card games are examples of something designed to incorporate randomness, and scores of other examples could be given. As computational biologist Joshua Swamidass explains, "The use of 'random' mutations in science is not a metaphysical claim about mutations arising independent of God's will or creative work. Instead, it is just a limited claim that these mutations are not predictable to scientists. 'Random' mutations, therefore, are no more a threat to religious belief than are the 'random' cast of dice in a casino."[4] Purpose and chance are not automatically incompatible, nor are they mutually exclusive.

Others contend that the randomness of the biological world only reveals that it is wasteful and meaningless. Consider the following statement by paleontologist, and atheist, Stephen Jay Gould: "Odd arrangement and funny solutions are the proof of evolution—paths that a sensible God would never tread but

---

[4] Joshua Swamidass, "Advancing Evolutionary Science in Dialogue with Islam," *Theology and Science* 21, no. 4 (November 22, 2023), 642–59, https://doi.org/10.1080/14746700.2023.2255949.

that a natural process, constrained by history, follows perforce."[5] In other words, the biological world appears to be too ridiculous and profligate to be the work of a God of reason.

I'm not sure what "sensible God" Gould had in mind, but it was not the God of the Bible—certainly not the Son of God who became one of us in the person of Jesus of Nazareth. As N. T. Wright points out, this world of seemingly inexplicable detours and wasteful extravagance is exactly what Jesus tells us we should expect. Wright explains:

> To begin with, if creation comes through the kingdom bringing Jesus, we ought to expect it be like a seed growing secretly. That it would involve seed being sown in a prodigal fashion in which a lot went to waste, apparently, but other seed producing a great crop. We ought to expect that it be like a strange, slow process which might suddenly reach some kind of harvest. We ought to expect that it would involve some kind of overcoming of chaos. Above all, we ought to expect that it would be a work of utter, self-giving love. That the power which made the world, like the power which ultimately rescued the world, would be the power not of brute force, but of radical, outpoured generosity. We ought to expect, in other words, that the creation would not look like an oriental despot deciding to build a palace, and just throwing it up at speed, with his architects and builders cowering before him. . . . But various scientists (not least the Darwin family a century before Charles

---

[5] Stephen Jay Gould, *The Panda's Thumb* (New York: W. W. Norton, 1980), 20–21.

> Darwin), motivated by quite a different worldview—namely, Epicureanism—nonetheless come up with a picture of Origins that looks remarkably like Jesus' parables of the Kingdom: some seeds go to waste, others bear remarkable fruit; some projects start tiny and take forever, but ultimately produce a great crop; some false starts are wonderfully rescued, others are forgotten. Chaos is astonishingly overcome.
>
> This says nothing about generosity, since that word only makes sense in terms of a personal creator. Which the Epicureans, like Erasmus Darwin, Charles's grandfather, had ruled out. That's one of the major differences, but the evolutionists were driven again and again to speak of the prodigality of the natural world. The theologian can pick that up and say, "Yes! Precisely what you would expect if there was a God of boundless, generous love behind it all. The prodigal father. The God we know in and as Jesus the Messiah.[6]

In his talk, "God Is an Artist," biochemist Fuz Rana covers many of these same themes as he marvels at the lavishness and extravagance in creation. Some things seem even frivolous. Rana gives example after example of bizarre and interesting creatures that show that God is not only the Engineer of history; he's also the Artist who delights in displaying his creative flair. Rana concludes his talk by declaring that "God is Baroque!"[7] (The

---

[6] N. T. Wright, "Christ and Creation: Exploring the Paradox," BioLogos, April 25, 2017, https://biologos.org/resources/if-creation-is-through-christ-evolution-is-what-you-would-expect.

[7] Fazale Rana, "God Is . . . an Artist," https://www.youtube.com/watch?v=x9UjscEoYig.

Baroque period was a time in which music, art, and architecture were noted for their over-the-top decorative excessiveness.)

Scientists study the material world and the processes that occur therein. From their studies they are able to discern the properties and relationships of those material processes—nothing more and nothing less. One thing they have discovered is that randomization is one of the primary processes in our world. The actions of mixing and scattering—what physicist John Polkinghorne calls "the shuffling explorations of potentiality"—play fundamental roles.[8] When we focus on details, it is difficult to discern any order or pattern. Chaos rules. However, when we look at the bigger picture, we discover surprising overall patterns and areas of order in unexpected places. In the field of biology, the concepts of purpose, function, and teleology are making a comeback.[9] (In biology, teleology is the view that the features of living creatures show evidence of purpose or intent—evidence from which one can infer a Divine Mind.)

What Is the Theory of Evolution?

So, with an appreciation of God's sovereign work over a seemingly messy world, let's consider Darwin's theory of evolution. Three common uses of the word *evolution* should be noted. First the word can simply mean *biological change over time*. The idea that the characteristics of a species can change over time

---

[8] John Polkinghorne, "Science and Theology in the Twenty-First Century, *Zygon* 35, no. 4 (December 2000): 947.

[9] Edward Feser, *Aristotle's Revenge: The Metaphysical Foundations of Physical and Biological Science* (Neunkirchen-Seelscheid: Editiones Scholasticae, 2019).

is not a controversial concept, and hardly anyone—including young-earth creationists—disagree with this definition of evolution. For example, there are hundreds of different dog breeds, with new breeds being developed regularly.

A second and more controversial use of the word *evolution* is to refer to *the theory of common descent*. This is the idea that all life on Earth shares a common ancestor. Evolutionists argue that we can see traces of shared traits and genetic materials across diverse groups of organisms. Evolutionists point to the commonality of certain features, namely the ubiquity of cells and DNA. Living things, from tiny bacteria to gigantic whales and even we humans, are all made up of cells. Just as every living thing either is a cell or is made up of cells, at the center of every cell is the DNA molecule. From the smallest bacterium to the biggest blue whale, the DNA molecule (which stands for deoxyribonucleic acid) is the central element driving every cell. This molecule serves as a blueprint, storing the information that determines the characteristics of a particular organism. DNA is universal—we've never found any living thing that doesn't have DNA. Proponents of common descent point to such universal features as cells and the DNA molecule as one line of evidence for common descent.

A third way the word *evolution* is used is in reference to the theory that adaptation occurs by means of natural section. Several biologists and naturalists in the nineteenth century proposed some version of evolutionary theory, but none of the theories provided a mechanism that could be the driving force behind evolution. That's what Darwin and Wallace's theory attempted to do—explain the process of evolution. They argued that natural selection was the engine. Organisms with traits best suited to their environment are more likely to survive and reproduce and, thus, pass on these advantageous traits to their offspring. Over time, this selecting process leads to adaptations that can result in new species. This theory of evolution by means of natural selection became known as Darwinism.

Yet even Darwinists conceded that the theory still had gaps. Namely the theory had no explanation for how variations came about in the first place or how those advantageous variations were retained. The discovery of genetics seemed to fill in those gaps. Random mutations in DNA provide variations, and then DNA retains the favorable variations chosen by natural selection. The combination of Darwinism with genetics in the first part of the twentieth century became known as Neo-Darwinism (or the "modern synthesis"), and these are its hallmarks: (1) random variation by means of genetic mutations, (2) favorable variations by means of natural selection, and (3) universal descent from a common ancestor.

But Neo-Darwinism also turned out to be woefully inadequate. Many biologists are now arguing for what is often called the "extended evolutionary synthesis" (EES). They recognize that Neo-Darwinism is overly simplistic and doesn't explain much of what we actually see in nature. For one thing, the fossil record doesn't support gradualism. Darwin acknowledged, "If it could be demonstrated that any complex organ existed, which could not possibly have been formed by numerous, successive, slight modifications, my theory would absolutely break down."[10] As the context makes clear, he did not expect this to

[10] Charles Darwin, *On the Origin of Species* (London: Murray, 1859), 189.

be a problem for his theory. However, rather than new species arriving via "numerous, successive, slight modifications," these new species seem to explode onto the scene. Paleontologists discern at least five such major biological "explosions," with the Cambrian explosion being the most notable.

Though some argue that EES is simply an expansion of the current evolutionary framework, others view it as a revolutionary break because EES challenges the fundamental assumptions of Neo-Darwinism, such as the primacy of gradual, random genetic change and the idea that natural selection is the primary driver of evolutionary innovation. Today, biologists recognize that the processes affecting living things are more complex than just natural selection or "survival of the fittest." Nor do genetic mutations produce new species. As University of Chicago microbiologist James A. Shapiro explains,

> A lot has changed since 1859. We now know that Darwin's "gradualist" view of evolution, exclusively driven by natural selection, is no longer compatible with contemporary science. It's not just that random mutations are one of many evolutionary processes that produce new species; they have nothing to do with the major evolutionary transformations of macroevolution. Species do not emerge from an accumulation of random genetic changes.[11]

Shapiro argues instead for a process he calls "natural genetic engineering" and calls on other biologists to recognize that cells

---

[11] James A. Shapiro, "Evolution without Accidents," ed. Cameron Allan McKean, *Aeon*, accessed November 28, 2023, https://aeon.co/essays/why-did-darwins-20th-century-followers-get-evolution-so-wrong.

show clear indications of teleology. The current models in biology are much more open to theistic interpretations than the Neo-Darwinist model that dominated the twentieth century.

The Three Major Christian Approaches to Biology

Are evolution and design compatible? Or to ask the question more precisely: Are some versions of evolutionary theory congruent with certain versions of design theory? The best minds in theology, philosophy, and science have debated this question ever since Darwin and Wallace presented their theory of evolution by means of natural selection.

In fact, Darwin and Wallace themselves disagreed. Darwin believed that their theory was incompatible with any notion of creation, design, or teleology. Wallace strongly believed otherwise, viewing evolution as how God benevolently created the universe (albeit Wallace's religious views were far from orthodox). Still, he argued that natural processes alone could not explain certain features, such as the human mind and speech.

The debate continues. At the extremes of the spectrum of views are Neo-Darwinism at one end and young-earth creationism (YEC) at the other. In between the two extremes are several mediating views, most notably old-earth creationism (OEC, also called progressive creationism) and evolutionary creationism (EC, also called theistic evolution).

Young-Earth Creationism

YEC proponents argue that the accepted chronology of the fossil record is wrong by many orders of magnitude. They contend that the geological column was created during the year of Noah's flood.[12] Interestingly, YEC advocates claim that the accepted rate of biological changes is also wrong by similar orders of magnitude—but this time in the opposite direction. They believe that there were only approximately 1,500 different air-breathing species or "kinds" on the ark.[13] An explosion of biological diversity occurred in the few hundred years after the flood, and this explosion explains the remarkable number of species that we see throughout the world today.

According to many YEC models, after the flood the species or "kinds" aboard the ark served as "proto-species" for the many species that developed as they adapted to the different environments to which they wandered. Thus, from an original "proto-canine" descended wolves, coyotes, and dogs; and from a "proto-feline" descended the broad family of lions, tigers, and other types of cats. Some of the conjectures made by YEC models are quite surprising: they suggest that from an original "proto-bovine" descended buffalo, bison, cows—and also sheep and goats.[14] The argument that cows, sheep, and goats share a common ancestor demonstrates that YEC proponents are much more amenable to speciation than is generally recognized.

---

[12] See John Whitcomb and Henry Morris, *The Genesis Flood: The Biblical Record and Its Scientific Implications, 50th Anniversary Edition* (Phillipsburg, PA: P&R, 2011).

[13] Ken Ham, "How Many Animals Were on Noah's Ark?," Answers in Genesis, September 8, 2022, https://answersingenesis.org/blogs/ken-ham/2022/09/08/how-many-animals-were-noahs-ark/.

[14] "Speciation," Answers in Genesis, accessed November 28, 2023, https://answersingenesis.org/natural-selection/speciation/.

Evolutionary Creationism

BioLogos is the leading apologetics ministry that argues for evolutionary creationism (or theistic evolution). They explain EC thus:

> ECs accept evolution as the best scientific explanation we have for how life on Earth has changed over time. In biology, evolution refers to "descent with modification," which includes the idea that all species are descended from a common ancestor over many generations. We therefore accept the scientific evidence that all life on Earth is related, including humans—which does not negate the image of God in us.[15]

The scientists, theologians, and other scholars at BioLogos endeavor to be faithful to both science and Scripture, and they are motivated by the conviction that evolution and the Bible are compatible.[16] But many, if not most, EC advocates deny a historical Adam and Eve.

Old-Earth Creationism

Like evolutionary creationism, old-earth creationism acknowledges the scientific consensus of an ancient universe and earth, accepting evidence such as the geological column, the

---

[15] "What Is Evolutionary Creation?," BioLogos, last updated February 6, 2024, https://biologos.org/common-questions/what-is-evolutionary-creation.

[16] See Deborah Haarsma and Loren Haarsma, *Origins: Christian Perspectives on Creation, Evolution, and Intelligent Design* (Grand Rapids, MI: Faith Alive Christian Resources, 2011).

radiometric dating of rocks, and cosmic background radiation. However, OEC challenges the standard Darwinian and Neo-Darwinian explanations (random mutations and natural selection) and argues that they don't adequately explain the geological and biological evidences.[17]

Old-earth creationism contends that God progressively created new life forms over the course of natural history. OEC asserts that while the mechanisms of evolution might explain microevolutionary changes within species, those mechanisms are insufficient to account for the macroevolutionary leaps between species and higher *taxa* (or groups). Therefore, these significant jumps in complexity are seen as evidence of hypernatural actions. It's important to note that OEC proponents do not claim to know how God involved himself in these significant hinge moments in natural history, but they do claim that the inference of the best explanation points to divine activity.

OEC proponents acknowledge that there is either an organic continuity between the species or an organic similarity among the species, but they argue strongly that natural processes are not sufficient to explain the empirical evidence. They contend that some type of supernatural and/or hypernatural action was necessary—particularly in the origin of humanity. Some OEC proponents hold that at times God intervened in natural history, using the existing species to bring about new species. Other OEC proponents argue that the major kinds were created *de novo* ("anew") and then developed into further species as they adapted to their respective environments. Not surprisingly, YEC advocates reject OEC views as a departure from Scripture.

---

[17] See Hugh Ross, *A Matter of Days: Resolving a Creation Controversy,* 2nd ed. (Covina, CA: RTB, 2015).

Nevertheless, one key feature of OEC is its insistence that humans are a unique creation, made by God in his image. While it recognizes the existence of hominids, it holds that modern humans (*Homo sapiens*) are a distinct creation. This aspect differentiates OEC from EC, which typically accepts human evolution as part of God's creation process. Progressive creationism also accepts the existence of animal death and suffering before the fall of man. This diverges also from the young-earth creationist view, which sees these phenomena as direct results of human sin. (As I noted before, this book is written from an OEC perspective.) Just as in other scientific fields, biology exhibits evidence of successive hypernatural divine actions.

Both evolutionary creationists (EC) and old-earth creationists (OEC) agree that the universe is finely tuned and that the earth is a very rare, very special place.[18] It seems that the difference between EC and OEC lies in where each sees special divine action occurring. EC argues that the universe was sufficiently front-loaded, rigged at the beginning, so that life was able to evolve in at least one place—earth. They would say that the hypernatural moment was the initial moment of the big bang. By contrast OEC argues that, in addition to the big bang, the fossil and genetic evidence indicate that a number of hypernatural actions can be detected at various stages of natural history.

Another area of agreement between EC and OEC is the view that naturalistic, Neo-Darwinian evolution alone does not have sufficient explanatory power to account for the world we see. EC proponents push back at the notion that they are

[18] By arguing that the universe is less than 10,000 years old, YEC takes itself out of the game at this point.

merely evolutionists. According to EC, evolution plus design (i.e., a divine ordering of the initial conditions) has greater explanatory power than evolution alone and, in fact, provides a sufficient explanation. OEC proponents disagree. They argue that the geological, biological, and biblical records indicate that at various times in natural history additional direct and immediate divine action occurred.

Biological fine-tuning seems to point, once again, to a world ordered carefully by an all-wise, all-powerful, and all-loving Designer. Two EC proponents are theologians Kirk MacGregor and E. V. Rope Kojonen. They both agree that the fossil record and genetic evidences indicate that some type of evolutionary processes have been at work. However, both also argue that if evolution is true, then that points to something akin to miraculous action.[19] In "Evolution as Evidence for God's Existence," MacGregor goes so far as to argue that evolution demonstrates the existence of God. He gives the following syllogism:

1. If biological evolution occurred, it would undoubtedly have been extraordinarily improbable, beyond scientific ability to explain *why* it happened (although science certainly has the ability to show *that* it happened).
2. By definition, events beyond scientific ability to explain why they happened constitutes miracles, whose reality demand the existence of God.
3. If biological evolution occurred, it would have been a miracle requiring the existence of God.

---

[19] E. V. R. Kojonen, *The Compatibility of Evolution and Design* (New York: Palgrace Macmillan, 2021), and Kirk MacGregor, *A Molinist-Anabaptist Systematic Theology* (Lanham, MD: University Press of America, 2007).

4. Beyond reasonable doubt genetic evidence primarily, and fossil evidence secondarily, establishes the reality of biological evolution (that evolution happened).
5. Beyond reasonable doubt, God exists.[20]

One does not have to fully embrace MacGregor's position to appreciate the force of his argument. Biology presents us with a hypernatural world. It's a world of complex natural processes that are interspersed with compelling evidences of special divine action. Biology presents us with a world that is designed to adapt.

---

[20] MacGregor, *A Molinist-Anabaptist Systematic Theology,* 183–7 (emphasis original).

9

The Believing Scientist

> We do not look for proof for God, because we already know from Jesus that He exists. Instead we enter science to worship, finding great awe and wonder in the beauty and mystery of it all.
>
> —James Tour

Charles Townes (1915–2015) was a renowned American physicist, a polymath noted for his research in a remarkable range of scientific fields. His accomplishments included work in the Apollo space program, advances in quantum mechanics, and help in the discovery of black holes. In 1964, he won the Nobel Prize in physics for his part in the invention of lasers. Townes was also a committed follower of Jesus, and his scientific colleagues knew that well.

In a chapter titled "Reflections on Life as a Physicist," he recounts his life's story, modestly talking about his achievements. He describes a life that was filled with both research and prayer, both scientific discovery and divine guidance. Townes ended with imagining that some reader might ask how, when, and where Townes perceived God to be working in his life. His answer: "If you believe in God at all, there is no particular 'where'; He's always here—everywhere. He's in all of these things. To me God is personal, yet omnipresent—a great source of strength. . . . When my atheistic friend asks, 'What has he done for you?' What can I say? I look at what's happened to me, and think that all of those things are what He's done."[1]

Townes understood his work in science to be his "vocation." The term *vocation* comes from the Latin word *vocatio*, which means "calling." Every Christian is called to a life of service to God by the gifts and abilities God bestows. If God has called you to serve him in one of the STEM fields (STEM stands for science, technology, engineering, and math), then the Bible gives clear instructions about how to fulfill your vocation: "Whatever you do, do it from the heart, as something done for the Lord and not for people, knowing that you will receive the reward of an inheritance from the Lord. You serve the Lord Christ" (Col 3:23–24). The believing scientist will face challenges, and it's important that he or she understands basic truths about Scripture, general revelation, the fall, and common grace. Most important, Jesus Christ must be at the center.

Scripture and Science

What is the proper role of the Bible in the life and thinking of a believing scientist? Protestants in general and evangelicals in

[1] Charles Townes, *Making Waves* (Woodbury, NY: American Institute of Physics Press, 1995), 203.

particular affirm *sola Scriptura*, the view that the Bible alone is the final authority in matters of faith and practice. Most evangelical theologians embrace some version of the Wesleyan Quadrilateral (Scripture, tradition, reason, and experience). Scripture has a magisterial role, while the other three have ministerial roles. Most evangelical scholars affirm that all four—Scripture, tradition, reason, and experience—have a role in forming our understanding, with Scripture overseeing the ministerial role of the other three.

Most evangelicals reject *nuda Scriptura* ("only Scripture" or "bare-naked Scripture") and *solo Scriptura* ("I alone reading Scripture"). Note: there is a big difference between *solo Scriptura* and *sola Scriptura*! "Solo" means that I don't need anyone else to help me understand the Bible and that I am the ultimate authority for what the Bible means to me. *Sola Scriptura* doesn't mean that we use only Scripture but, rather, that we have all the Scripture we need. We utilize a lot of truth that is not in Scripture (e.g., 2 + 2 = 4 is not in the Bible). Nor do we affirm *solo Scriptura*. Nobody is a theological *tabula rasa* ("blank slate"). I cannot think of a current evangelical theologian who affirms either *nuda Scriptura* or *solo Scriptura*. *Sola Scriptura* does not mean simply "Scripture only." Rather, *sola Scriptura* means "Scripture primarily," "Scripture above," or "Scripture ultimately."

Evangelicals also affirm the sufficiency of Scripture, which is the belief that the Bible is able to equip believers for every good work (2 Tim 3:17). The word *sufficient* should indicate to us that this is actually a modest claim. Scripture is sufficient. That is, it is adequate; it is enough. It is not exhaustive or comprehensive in stating everything that could be stated.

For example, the Bible doesn't teach brain surgery, but it does provide clear teaching so that a brain surgeon can come to a saving knowledge of Jesus Christ and know how to follow him in a life of believing obedience. So, while affirming Scripture's sufficiency is a modest claim, it is this modesty that gives the doctrine its power.

Scripture provides the conceptual context sufficient for living out any area and vocation of life. Scripture does not provide the content. Scripture is sufficient for the particle physicist and the biochemist, not because the Bible gives pertinent information relevant to either area of study but because the Bible informs the worldview that makes such scientific endeavors possible. John Frame explains, "Scripture contains divine words sufficient for all of life. It has all the divine words that the plumber needs, and all the divine words that the theologian needs. So it is just as sufficient for plumbing as it is for theology. And in that sense it is sufficient for science and ethics as well."[2] Frame has it right. Scripture is sufficient for everything from home improvements to genetic engineering, but the concomitant doctrines of general revelation, the fall, and common grace must also be brought into the conversation.

General Revelation

The Bible affirms the reality of general revelation. At least, the consensus view is that it does. Passages such as Psalm 19, Acts 17, and Romans 1–2 all seem to teach that God communicates in

---

[2] John M. Frame, *The Doctrine of the Word of God* (Phillipsburg, PA: P&R, 2010), 221.

a general sense to all. In a way, general revelation is similar to the image of God. Scripture affirms the existence of both, but it does not elaborate about either of them as to what exactly they are.

When examining the nature of general revelation, scholars typically note that the Bible indicates that general revelation occurs at three levels. The broadest, highest level is cosmic revelation (e.g., "The heavens declare the glory of God," Ps 19:1). The next, intermediate level is providential revelation (e.g., Paul speaks of God showing his hand in human history in Acts 17). The third level is the most personal and intimate—the human conscience (e.g., Paul speaks of those without the law as yet having the law "written on their hearts" in Rom 2:15). Christians believe in the existence of this three-tier telescoping general revelation because special revelation teaches us that it exists.

The Impact of the Fall and the Effects of Original Sin

While the church has affirmed the presence of a universal, general revelation, it also has recognized an equally universal obstacle. This obstacle is the ongoing impact of ancestral sin. Adam and Eve enjoyed an immediate access to God that humanity today does not. Not only has humanity just been expelled from the garden, but humanity's inclinations have been twisted, its loves disordered, its volitions rendered rebellious and idolatrous, and its cognitive abilities and rational processes darkened and damaged. The human race resides in a state of spiritual death. Typically, we group these detrimental effects under the heading of original sin.

The creation account says that God created humanity in his image and in his likeness (Gen 1:26). Many patristic church fathers and medieval theologians made a distinction between the divine image and the divine likeness. "Image" referred to those natural, essential traits such as rationality and volition. "Likeness" was understood to mean those ways that humans could be morally godly (i.e., qualities such as faithfulness and holiness). These qualities were accidental (i.e., nonessential) properties that were lost in the fall. This approach understood humans to have lost the divine likeness, but the divine image remained intact.

The Reformers understood image and likeness to be an example of Hebrew parallelism, thus the terms *image* and *likeness* are synonyms. This means, in the Protestant view, the whole person has been affected by the fall. Therefore, divine image, while not erased or removed, has been disastrously marred. This is what is meant by the term *total depravity*—not that humans are always as bad as they completely can be but that the fall affected every aspect of the human person (including mind and will). Most Old Testament scholars today agree with the exegesis of the Reformers.

Interestingly, the doctrine of the fall played a significant role in the rise of modern science. Historian Peter Harrison has demonstrated that the scientists of the sixteenth and seventeenth centuries were convinced that Adam's original cognitive abilities were far superior to those humans have today.[3] Those pristine and unencumbered faculties were seriously damaged and curtailed by the primeval event. The development of the

[3] Peter Harrison, *The Fall of Man and the Foundations of Science* (Cambridge: Cambridge University Press, 2007).

scientific method and the utilization of scientific instruments were viewed as means to ameliorating the present, truncated human condition.

The Benevolent Effects of Common Grace

The Bible teaches that there exists a general revelation, available to everyone, everywhere at all times. That's the good news. Unfortunately, this universal revelation is universally resisted due to the universal effects of original sin. That's the bad news. If that were the end of the matter, then this story would end on a very sour note. However, the subsequent good news is that there also exists a universal, common grace. This grace works in tandem with God's general providence to enable damaged, dysfunctional humans to still reflect flashes of the One who created them—sometimes brilliantly.

It should be noted that most discussions about general revelation and common grace have centered primarily, but not exclusively, on theological issues rather than scientific matters. That is, most explorations have focused on questions such as the knowledge of God and the possibility of salvation. The church fathers were intrigued more by Plato's and Aristotle's theological insights concerning the nature of God than they were about these two philosophers' explorations of the natural world.

This is not to say that the church fathers' discussions about common grace were exclusively about theology. They believed that the Divine Logos illuminated the entire world (e.g., John 1:9) and that the Holy Spirit worked universally to restrain humanity from its worst inclinations (e.g., 2 Thess 2:6–7). This ubiquitous work enables all humans, regardless of spiritual condition, to grasp the world around them. Thus according to

Augustine, "The divine Light serves as the basis not only for the intuitive grasp of the principles of logic and number, but also for apparently intuitive judgments of beauty in craft, art, music, poetry, or rhetoric, and for judgments of value in law and ethics."[4] The Bible presents common grace as operating through the covenants that God made to Adam (Gen 1:26–28) and Noah (Gen 9:1–16). These first two covenants were given to all humanity, and they bequeath to all humans the temporal blessings of the dominion mandate but not eternal salvation.[5] Thus, humanity as a whole—not just redeemed humanity—has made extraordinary strides in acquiring knowledge of the natural world.

How are we to go about engaging with our knowledge of the natural world? The majority view of the early church fathers seems to be that Christians, with due caution and in community, can "plunder the Egyptians." This is because, as Augustine explains, "all truth is God's truth."[6]

> But whether the fact is as Varro has related, or is not so, still we ought not to give up music because of the superstition of the heathen, if we can derive anything from it that is of use for the understanding of Holy Scripture; nor does it follow that we must busy ourselves with their theatrical trumpery because we enter upon an

[4] J. Patout Burns, "Grace," in *Augustine through the Ages: An Encyclopedia*, ed. Allan D. Fitzgerald (Grand Rapids, MI: Eerdmans, 1999), 392.

[5] Gerald L. Bray, "Grace," in *New Dictionary of Theology: Historical and Systematic*, ed. Martin Davie et al. (Wheaton, IL: IVP, 2016), 377.

[6] A common paraphrase of Augustine, *On Christian Doctrine*, 2.18, https://www.newadvent.org/fathers/12022.htm.

> investigation about harps and other instruments, that may help us to lay hold upon spiritual things. For we ought not to refuse to learn letters because they say that Mercury discovered them; nor because they have dedicated temples to Justice and Virtue, and prefer to worship in the form of stones things that ought to have their place in the heart, ought we on that account to forsake justice and virtue. *Nay, but let every good and true Christian understand that wherever truth may be found, it belongs to his Master* [emphasis added]; and while he recognizes and acknowledges the truth, even in their religious literature, let him reject the figments of superstition, and let him grieve over and avoid men who, "when they knew God, glorified him not as God, neither were thankful; but became vain in their imaginations, and their foolish heart was darkened. Professing themselves to be wise, they became fools, and changed the glory of the incorruptible God into an image made like to corruptible man, and to birds, and four-footed beasts, and creeping things."[7]

When properly applied, Augustine's adage—"all truth is God's truth"—can guide a believer in whatever vocational endeavor he or she is called.

How do we approach STEM research disciplines that may have non-Christian origins, that may be dominated by non-Christian thought leaders, or that may be utilized by opponents to argue against the Christian faith? For a nonscientific example, consider the works of Karl Marx. In his study of

[7] Augustine, 2.18.28.

economic theory, Marx began from a perspective of dialectical materialism. He argued for the superiority and the eventual triumph of communism. His starting assumptions are wrong, and his conclusions are equally wrong. However, it must be acknowledged that, in between, Marx's observations about life in the early days of the Industrial Revolution are astute and perceptive.[8] Embedded within so much error are flashes of brilliant insight.

Many similar examples can be found in the scientific community. There are scientists who, starting from a materialist worldview, conclude that the cosmos shows no evidence of purpose or design, but their explorations of the empirical evidence display intelligence and even genius. The task of "plundering the Egyptians" is one that must be done with care, but it is a necessary one. Scripture is a sufficient guide to the believing scientist in this worthwhile endeavor, but the process of properly applying biblical authority must be done wisely.

Believing scientists are called to be engaged in the disciplined exploration of God's creation. This exploration is also an interpretative process. We believe that Scripture is sufficient for the scientific enterprise because the Bible provides sufficient certainty about God's will for us in this world. Scripture (1) presents us with an understanding of reality sufficient to engage in the scientific, interpretative process; (2) provides a sufficient rationale of, and justification for, exploring the world; (3) sufficiently affirms confidence in our ability to perceive reality; (4) mandates sufficient guidelines for conducting all such explorations in an

[8] See for example, Karl Marx, *Capital: A Critique of Political Economy,* vol. 1 (New York: Penguin Classics, 1992).

ethical manner; and (5) gives sufficient criteria for evaluating the metaphysical implications of the resultant discoveries. "The sufficiency of Scripture" is a modest yet powerful concept.

A Word about Concordism and Congruence

The claim of Scripture's sufficiency to guide believing scientists raises questions generally associated with concordism. John Soden defines *concordism* as "the position that the teaching of the Bible on the natural world, properly interpreted, will agree with the teaching of science (when it properly understands the data), and may in fact supplement science."[9] Most involved in the faith and science dialogue recognize strong and moderate (or hard and soft) versions of concordism. Strong concordism views the Bible as teaching scientific knowledge that otherwise was not available in ancient times. Moderate concordism views the Bible as God accommodating both the content and language of his revelation to the people at the time it was given. God revealed what could be understood then, even if it might be revealed differently now.

Concordism has received substantial criticism lately in conservative evangelical circles. Whatever evangelicals may think about the level and nature of scientific concordism, it seems necessary to affirm at least some type of historical concordism. Historical concordism is understood to mean that the Bible is true in all its historical claims and affirmations—and this includes claims about natural history.

---

[9] "Concordism," in *Dictionary of Christianity and Science*, ed. Paul Copan et al. (Grand Rapids, MI: Zondervan, 2017), 104.

Concerning scientific matters, perhaps *congruence* rather than *concordism* would be a more helpful or accurate term. Congruence makes the more modest claim that, properly understood, the teachings of Scripture and the findings of science coincide, agree, or harmonize easily. For example, *creatio ex nihilo* is congruent with the big bang theory (i.e., they fit together well in that both affirm that all that now exists had a beginning in the past). But congruence doesn't claim that Gen 1:1 specifically predicted that the universe is 13.8 billion years old. Likewise, the Bible describes the world as being lovingly prepared and providentially cared for. These characterizations are congruent with the fine-tuning and the Rare Earth hypotheses. Similarly, Scripture presents God as actively creating, in an incremental, step-by-step fashion (Gen 1:2–26). This is congruent with the scientific finding that there is a progression to life in the fossil record, but this progression resists purely naturalistic explanations. The evidences of purpose, function, and rational intention are congruent with the teleological emphasis of Scripture.

Jesus Christ at the Center

The New Testament presents Jesus of Nazareth as the Lord and Savior of the world. It grounds those claims first and foremost in Jesus's relationship to creation. The Bible declares that Jesus is the Creator, Sustainer, and Purpose of the universe. The apostle John opened his Gospel with the declaration that Jesus Christ created all things: "In the beginning was the Word, and the Word was with God, and the Word was God. He was with God in the beginning. All things were created through him, and apart from him not one thing was created that has been created" (John 1:1–3). Throughout the New Testament, the other apostles agree with John's presentation of Jesus as Creator (Col 1:15–17; Heb 1:1–4). In addition to creating the world, Paul made the additional claim that Jesus Christ actively and continuously sustains all things. He declared, "He is before all things, and by him all things hold together" (Col 1:17).

This means that the universe is not self-sustaining or self-perpetuating. We continue to exist because the Son of God wills us to do so. If he were to stop, then we would return to where we came from—to nothing. We would cease to be. Fortunately for us, "Jesus Christ is the same yesterday, today, and forever" (Heb 13:8). In his letter to the Ephesians, Paul explains how Jesus Christ is the goal of all things: "He made known to us the mystery of his will, according to his good pleasure that he purposed in Christ as a plan for the right time—to bring everything together in Christ, both things in heaven and things on earth in him" (Eph 1:9–10). The Son of God, the Second Person of the triune Godhead, took on flesh in the virgin Mary's womb. He became the man who was Jesus of Nazareth. He is the One who lived, died, and rose again. For the Christian he is our salvation, our example, and our Lord.

Whether we are scientists, taxi drivers, or any other vocation, Jesus claims us and calls us to follow him. One of the oldest prayers of the early church of which we have record is ascribed to the missionary to Ireland, Saint Patrick. These beautiful ancient words seem especially appropriate for the Christian involved in one of the STEM fields. Patrick begins with a contemplation of the world God has created:

I arise today, through
The strength of heaven,
The light of the sun,
The radiance of the moon,
The splendor of fire,
The speed of lightning,
The swiftness of wind,
The depth of the sea,
The stability of the earth,
The firmness of rock.

Patrick's thoughts then move from creation to the One who created all things. His prayer reflects on the relationship Christ has to various elements of creation and human experience. By doing so, Patrick acknowledges Christ's omnipresence and his intimate connection with the world, then Patrick seeks a Christ-filled life:

I arise today . . .
Christ with me, Christ before me, Christ behind me,
Christ in me, Christ beneath me, Christ above me,
Christ on my right, Christ on my left,
Christ when I lie down, Christ when I sit down,
Christ in the heart of every man who thinks of me,
Christ in the mouth of everyone who speaks of me,
Christ in the eye that sees me,
Christ in the ear that hears me.

The Irish saint concludes his prayer in a way that relates creation to Christ and, ultimately, to the triune God:

I arise today
Through a mighty strength, the invocation of the Trinity,
Through a belief in the Threeness,
Through confession of the Oneness
of the Creator of creation.[10]

In this world Christ is with us. May your scientific explorations be expressions of worship.

---

[10] Saint Patrick, Lorica of Saint Patrick, EWTN, accessed November 28, 2023, https://www.ewtn.com/catholicism/devotions/lorica-of-saint-patrick-349.

SUBJECT INDEX

J

K

L

M

T

U

V

W

Y

Z

SCRIPTURE INDEX